Freelance Digital Marketing

By Humera Shazia

This Book is Dedicated to My Mother.

Table of Contents

Chapter 1 10

What is Marketing 10

    Definition 10

    Purpose of Marketing 11

    Types of Marketing 11

Evolution of Marketing 12

    What Causes Marketing To Evolve? 13

    Different Stages in the Evolution of Marketing 13

    The Production Era:1900-1930s. 14

    Products Develop from the Primordial Soup 14

    The Sales Era:1930s-1960s. 14

    Species Diverge and Brands Emerge in Marketing 14

    The Marketing Era:1960s-1980s. 15

    Intelligent Adaptations Focus on Meeting Customer Needs 15

    The Relationship Marketing Era: 1980-Present. 16

    Customers and Businesses Coevolve to Create Cooperative Societies .. 16

What is digital marketing 17

    Why is digital marketing important? 17

The benefits of digital marketing 18

- A broad geographic reach 18
- Cost efficiency 18
- Quantifiable results 18
- Easier personalization 19
- More connection with customers 19
- Easy and convenient conversions 20

B2B versus B2C digital marketing 20
What is digital media? 21
Types of digital marketing 21
- Search engine optimization 21
- Content marketing 22
- Social media marketing 23
- Pay-per-click marketing 25
- Affiliate marketing 25
- Native advertising 26
- Influencer marketing 27
- Marketing automation 27
- Email marketing 28
- Mobile marketing 29

Creating a digital marketing strategy 29
  a) Set SMART goals 29
  b) Identify your audience 29
  c) Create a budget 30
  d) Select your digital marketing channels 30
  e) Refine your marketing efforts 30

Power of digital marketing 30
How Has Digital Marketing Helped In This Era? 31
  a) Easily Accessible 31
  b) Refining Strategy 31
  c) The Level Of Play Is Same Regardless Of The Brand 32
  d) Greater Exposure 32
  e) Use A Reliable Digital Marketing Agency 32

Chapter 2 34
Important characteristics to be successful Digital Marketer 34
- The Ability to Self-Start 35
- Loving a Challenge 35

- Flexibility and Adaptability 35
- A Passion for Learning 36
- The Desire to Help Grow Other Businesses 36
- Communication Skills 37
- Leadership and Management Skills 37
- Trustworthiness, Reliability, and Dedication 37
- Strategic and Analytical Thinking 38

Popular Digital Marketing Jargons to learn 38

Chapter 3 44

Freelancing as a Digital Marketer 44

What is Freelancing? 44
What are the advantages of being a freelancer? 45
a) Flexibility to decide how, when and where to work 45
b) Choosing your own clients 45
c) Keeping all the profits 46

Famous Freelancing Websites to Find Work 46
Digital Marketing for freelancers 47

Digital marketing Skills for non-Technical freelancers 48
1. Community Management: 48
1. Posting Skills 49
2. Advertising skills: 49
3. Acquisitions: 49
4. Performance Measurement: 49
5. Client Dealing: 49
6. Blog Creation: 49

Should You Become a Freelance Digital Marketer? 49
The Benefits of Freelance Digital Marketing 50
The Downsides of Being a Freelance Digital Marketer 50

Digital marketing tools to help you grow as a freelancer 51
Top 10 Best Digital Marketing Tools 51

1. MailChimp 52
2. Google Analytics 52
3. Google Ads 53
4. Canva Business 54
5. Trello 54
6. Slack 55
7. Yoast SEO 56
8. Survey Anyplace 56
9. Ahrefs 57
10. SEMRUSH 57

Chapter: 4 59

Freelance digital marketer 59
What are the pros and cons of freelance digital marketing? 61
Pros 61
Cons 61
How much do freelance digital marketers make? 62
What are the different digital marketing jobs you can do? 63
1) Facebook and Instagram ads 63
2) SEO consulting 63
3) Chatbots and customer service 63
4) Sales funnels and landing pages 63
5) PPC and Google Ads 64
How to get started as a digital marketing freelancer 64
1. Take a course to study what's new 65
2. Determine your skills 65
3. Pick your specializations 65
4. Find expert help for ongoing support 66
5. Follow blogs that focus on your specialty 66
6. Create your profile 67
7. Start applying for entry-level jobs 67

How to Become a Freelance Digital Marketer Pro? 68
- Step 1: Choose Your Marketing Specialties.................................. 68
- Step 2: Build Your Brand 68
- Step 3: Legally Register Your Brand 69
- Step 4: Level up Your Business and Entrepreneurship Skills 69
- Step 5: Establish a System for Creating Proposals 69
- Step 6: Set Your Pricing Strategy 70
- Step 7: Join Freelance Platforms Such as Fiverr and Upwork 70
- Step 8: Promote Your Freelance Work Availability on LinkedIn 70
- Step 9: Connect With Other Freelancers for Advice 71
- Step 10: Build a Loyal Customer Base 71
- Step 11: Organize Your Time 71
- Step 12: Monitor Cash Flow 71

Chapter 5: 72

Freelance Operations 72

How To Manage Your Freelance Business 72
What Does a Freelance Digital Marketer Do Every Day? 73
Create the Perfect Freelancer Daily Routine 73
1. Create a schedule and stick to it 74
2. Create Dedicated Office Space at Home 76
3. Dress for Work Like You're Going to the Office 77

Time Management Tips for Freelancers 78
- **Create Processes** 78
- **Outsourcing** 79
- **Recurring Billing** 79

Common Freelance Mistakes to Avoid 79
- Freelance Mistake #1 - Scope Creep: The Silent Killer 80
- Freelance Mistake #2 - Having Only One Client 81
- Freelance Mistake #3 - Picking the Wrong Clients 81

Chapter 6 83

Finding, Negotiating and Managing clients 83
   How to find and communicate with your clients.............................83
   Negotiation Skills 84
      1. To claim value 84
      2. To offer the best value..85
      3. To form strategic partnerships..85
      4. To hire the best talent 86
      5. To attract lucrative offers..86
      6. To outperform the competition 87
      7. To improve marketing services 88
   Client Retention - How To Keep Your Freelance Clients Happy.........88
   Why Freelance Client Retention Is So Important 89
   Fix Retention Before Bringing on More Clients 90
      Freelancing Business VS Freelancing Side Hustle 91
   How to Keep the Scope of Your Project in Check? 95
   Managing Client Expectations (Promise Low, Deliver High) 97
      Managing Client Expectations - Tip # 1 97
      Managing Client Expectations - Tip # 2 98
      Managing Client Expectations - Tip # 3 98
      Managing Client Expectations - Tip # 4 99
   How to Send Deliverables to Your Clients...99
   Follow Up With Your Clients 100
   Meet Project Deadlines 100
   The Dos and Don'ts of Contracts and SOWs 101
   Dos: 101
   Don'ts: 101
   Deliver Results and Show Progress..102
   Deliver Real Results and Always Add Value 102
   Track Progress 104
   Learn When To Say "NO" 105
Definitions:..106

References: 110

Chapter 1
Basics

What is Marketing

Marketing is currently defined by the American Marketing Association (AMA) as "the activity, set of institutions, and processes for creating, communicating, delivering, and exchanging offerings that have value for customers, clients, partners, and society at large".

Definition

Dictionary.com defines marketing as, "the action or business of promoting and selling products or services, including market research and advertising."

According to Hub spot,

"Marketing refers to any actions a company takes to attract an audience to the company's product or services through high-quality messaging. Marketing aims to deliver standalone value for prospects and consumers through content, with the long-term goal of demonstrating product value, strengthening brand loyalty, and ultimately increasing sales."

The purpose of marketing is to research and analyze your consumers all the time, conduct focus groups, send out surveys, study online shopping habits, and ask one underlying question: "Where, when, and how does our consumer want to communicate with our business?"

Purpose of Marketing

Marketing is the process of getting people interested in your company's product or service. This happens through market research, analysis, and understanding your ideal customer's interests. Marketing pertains to all aspects of a business, including product development, distribution methods, sales, and advertising.

Types of Marketing

Where your marketing campaigns live depends entirely on where your customers spend their time. It's up to you to conduct market research that determines which types of marketing -- and which mix of tools within each type -- is best for building your brand. Here are several types of marketing that are relevant today, some of which have stood the test of time:

Internet marketing: Internet marketing (also known as online marketing, e-marketing, or web marketing,) is an all-inclusive term used to describe marketing activities conducted online. For this reason, internet marketing encompasses a wide range of strategies and tactics, such as social media marketing, content marketing, pay-per-click, and search engine optimization.

Search engine optimization: Abbreviated "SEO," this is the process of optimizing content on a website so that it appears in search engine results. It's used by marketers to attract people who perform searches to find particular products or services.

Blog marketing: Brands publish blogs to write about their industry and develop the interest of potential customers who browse the internet for specific information.

Social media marketing: Businesses can use Facebook, Instagram, Twitter, LinkedIn, and similar social networks to create impressions on their audience over time.

Print marketing: As newspapers and magazines get better at understanding who subscribes to their print material, businesses continue to sponsor articles, photography, and similar content in the publications their customers are reading.

Search engine marketing: This type of marketing is a bit different than SEO, which is described above. Businesses can now pay a search engine to place links on pages of its index that get high exposure to their audience. It's also called "pay-per-click.

Video marketing: Video Marketing is creating and publishing all kinds of videos that entertain and educate their core customers.

Evolution of Marketing

Marketing evolution refers to the distinct phases that businesses have gone through as they continued to seek new and innovative ways to achieve, maintain and increase revenue through customer sales and partnerships.

Since the 1900s, a variety of different strategies have been employed as various industries created and refined their marketing approaches.

The notion of different eras of marketing was first introduced by Robert Keith in his article "The Marketing Revolution" published in the Journal of Marketing in 1960.

What Causes Marketing to Evolve?

Two central factors drive marketing evolution:

- **Marketing technology:** When the field began, illustrated print advertising was one of the only feasible communication channels available to marketers besides in-store merchandising and in-person interactions. Today, digital marketing leverages technologies ranging from multimedia text messages to email and more.

- **Customer needs:** What do consumers demand today that they didn't yesterday? What can they afford now that was beyond their reach in the past? If you can't keep up with your audience, your competitors definitely will.

Different Stages in the Evolution of Marketing

For our purposes, we'll discuss four distinct phases of marketing evolution. While experts are somewhat divided in their interpretations of the various strategies that marketers have used to connect products with consumers and vice versa, we think these are the most important steps to study:

1. The Production Era
2. The Sales Era
3. The Marketing Era
4. The Relationship Era

The Production Era: 1900-1930s.

Products Develop from the Primordial Soup

The Industrial Revolution set the stage for modern marketing. All of the right ingredients were amassed, resulting in marketing as we now know it: the promotion of mass-produced consumer products.

Accordingly, early marketing efforts assumed a production orientation. The working theory was that customers simply needed to be informed about what goods were available to them. After all, you can't buy something if you don't know it exists.

The production era, up to the 1930s, is characterized by an abundance of raw materials and new mechanical processes that fueled an investment into mass production. Many companies concentrated on producing one single item. Marketing efforts generally consisted of informational brochures and catalogs.

The Sales Era: 1930s-1960s.

Species Diverge and Brands Emerge in Marketing

Leveraging a production orientation is fine if you're the only one in town. From the 1930s onward, it became increasingly rare that any company would permanently enjoy a competitor-free environment. So, in response to the pressures of natural selection, businesses developed unique adaptations. This resulted in two core innovations of modern marketing:

- the central importance of brand identities and
- an emphasis on the selling orientation

In the sales era, which ran from the 1930s to the 1960s, companies began to get more aggressive in their search for a competitive edge. Sales campaigns were devised to persuade customers or the advantages of the specific product over others. The customer's wants and needs became important and distribution networks were developed.

The Marketing Era:1960s-1980s.

Intelligent Adaptations Focus on Meeting Customer Needs

The development of a marketing orientation represented something of a big change. While traditional marketing had focused on simply getting products to customers and convincing them to buy, this new approach was different. Marketers were driven to better understand consumers' needs, concerns and desires. Only then could businesses hope to truly make an impact.

Brand marketing emerged during 1950s to the 1960s. In marketing departments, the brand manager emerged as the individual responsible for all marketing activities associated with a brand, and competition increased.

The Relationship Marketing Era: 1980-Present.

Customers and Businesses Coevolve to Create Cooperative Societies

Today employing a relationship orientation to marketing is common practice for many businesses. As a marketing concept, Relationship marketing is an approach that focuses on encouraging customer retention and loyalty as well as continued interaction with the brand. Digital marketing channels make it easy to deliver re-engagement incentives to consumers, and social media campaigns make brands highly accessible. Social responsibility can also be a cornerstone of this orientation, as brands strive to be perceived as a partner in the customer's quest to create a more equitable society.

The success of new social media platforms also highlights the importance of encouraging interaction among consumers. Instead of focusing solely on relationships between the business and its customers, companies will find new ways to participate constructively and collaboratively within a larger ecosystem led by consumers.

Evolution doesn't just stop. In the future, new approaches to product, customer and brand positioning will lead to novel marketing approaches that form the next stage of the evolution in the field. As always, new technology and shifting customer needs will lead to new approaches in marketing. The continued adoption of augmented reality (AR) and virtual reality (VR) will allow savvy innovators to create increasingly immersive experiences.

What is digital marketing

Digital marketing, also called online marketing, is the promotion of brands to connect with potential customers using the internet and other forms of digital communication. This includes not only email, social media, and web-based advertising, but also text and multimedia messages as a marketing channel.

In simple words, Digital marketing is all marketing activities that are done on modern digital channels. Those Marketing Activities are

- Paid Advertisement (TV Ads, website ads)
- Social Media Marketing (Facebook, YouTube, Instagram Ads)
- Email and SMS Marketing, WhatsApp Marketing
- Search Engine Optimization SEO
- Mobile Marketing
- Marketing Research

Digital Marketing has three core elements:

1. **Mass Reach:** A company can reach to millions of people through digital media.
2. **Interactivity:** Customers can interact and provide live feedback to the company on advertisements.
3. **Social Networking:** A community forum can be formed based on any interest.

Why is digital marketing important?

Any type of marketing can help your business thrive. However, digital marketing has become increasingly important because of how accessible digital channels are. In fact, there were 5 billion internet users globally in April 2022 alone.

From social media to text messages, there are many ways to use digital marketing tactics in order to communicate with your target audience. Additionally, digital marketing has minimal upfront costs, making it a cost-effective marketing technique for small businesses.

The benefits of digital marketing

Digital marketing has become prominent largely because it reaches such a wide audience of people. However, it also offers a number of other advantages that can boost your marketing efforts. These are a few of the benefits of digital marketing.

- ## A broad geographic reach

When you post an ad online, people can see it no matter where they are (provided you haven't limited your ad geographically). This makes it easy to grow your business's market reach and connect with a larger audience across different digital channels.

- ## Cost efficiency

Digital marketing not only reaches a broader audience than traditional marketing but also carries a lower cost. Overhead costs for newspaper ads, television spots, and other traditional marketing opportunities can be high. They also give you less control over whether your target audiences will see those messages in the first place.

With digital marketing, you can create just one content piece that draws visitors to your blog as long as it's active. You can create an email marketing campaign that delivers messages to targeted customer lists on a schedule, and it's easy to change that schedule or the content if you need to do so.

When you add it all up, digital marketing gives you much more flexibility and customer contact for your ad spend.

- ## Quantifiable results

To know whether your marketing strategy works, you have to find out how many customers it attracts and how much revenue it ultimately drives. But you cannot do that with a non-digital marketing method. With digital marketing, there's always the traditional option of asking each customer, "How did you find us?"

With digital marketing, results monitoring is simple. Digital marketing software and platforms automatically track the number of desired conversions that you get, whether that means email open rates, visits to your home page, or direct purchases.

- ## Easier personalization

Digital marketing allows you to gather customer data in a way that offline marketing can't. Data collected digitally tends to be much more precise and specific.

Imagine you offer financial services and want to send out special offers to internet users people who have looked at your products. You know you'll get better results if you target the offer to the person's interest, so you decide to prepare 2 campaigns. One is for young families who have looked at your life insurance products, and the other is for millennial entrepreneurs who have considered your retirement plans.

- How do you gather all of that data without automated tracking?
- How many phone records would you have to go through?
- How many customer profiles? And
- How do you know who has or hasn't read the brochure you sent out?

With digital marketing, all of this information is already at your fingertips.

- ## More connection with customers

Digital marketing lets you communicate with your customers in real-time. More importantly, it lets them communicate with you. Think about your social media strategy. It's great when your target audience sees your latest post, but it's even better when they can comment on it or share it. It means more buzz surrounding your product or service, as well as increased visibility every time someone joins the conversation.

Interactivity benefits your customers as well. Their level of engagement increases as they become active participants in your brand's story. That sense of ownership can create a strong sense of brand loyalty.

- **Easy and convenient conversions**

Digital marketing lets your customers take action immediately after viewing your ad or content. With traditional advertisements, the most immediate result you can hope for is a phone call shortly after someone views your ad. But how often does someone have the time to reach out to a company while they're doing the dishes, driving down the highway, or updating records at work?

With digital marketing, they can click a link or save a blog post and move along the sales funnel right away. They might not make a purchase immediately, but they'll stay connected with you and give you a chance to interact with them further.

B2B versus B2C digital marketing

Digital marketing strategies work for B2B (business to business) as well as B2C (business to consumer) companies, but best practices differ significantly between the two. Here's a closer look at how digital marketing is used in B2B and B2C marketing strategies.

B2B clients tend to have longer decision-making processes, and thus longer sales funnels. Relationship-building strategies work better for these clients, whereas B2C customers tend to respond better to short-term offers and messages.

B2B transactions are usually based on logic and evidence, which is what skilled B2B digital marketers present. B2C content is more likely to be emotionally-based, focusing on making the customer feel good about a purchase.

B2B decisions tend to need more than one person's input. The marketing materials that best drive these decisions tend to be shareable and downloadable. B2C customers, on the other hand, favor one-on-one connections with a brand.

Of course, there are exceptions to every rule. A B2C company with a high-ticket product, such as a car or computer, might offer more informative and serious content. As a result, your digital marketing strategy always needs to be geared toward your own customer base, whether you're B2B or B2C.

What is digital media?

Digital Media Refers to audio, video, photos or textual content that has been encoded using a computer or a smart device and can be **transmitted digitally** to people. For example

- An SMS for SMS Marketing,
- A video for YouTube marketing, and
- A post or Picture or video for Facebook Marketing

are examples of digital Media.

Types of digital marketing

There are as many specializations within digital marketing as there are ways of interacting using digital media. Here are a few key examples of types of digital marketing tactics.

- ## Search engine optimization

Search engine optimization, or SEO, is technically a marketing tool rather than a form of marketing in itself. The Balance defines it as "the art and science of making web pages attractive to search engines."

The "art and science" part of SEO is what's most important. SEO is a science because it requires you to research and weigh different contributing factors to achieve the highest possible ranking on a search engine results page (SERP).

Today, the most important elements to consider when optimizing a web page for search engines include:

- Quality of content
- Level of user engagement
- Mobile-friendliness
- Number and quality of inbound links

In addition to the elements above, you need to optimize **technical SEO**, which is all the back-end components of your site. This includes URL structure, loading times, and broken links. Improving your technical SEO can help search engines better navigate and crawl your site.

The strategic use of these factors makes search engine optimization a science, but the unpredictability involved makes it an art.

Ultimately, the goal is to rank on the first page of a search engine's result page. This ensures that those searching for a specific query related to your brand can easily find your products or services. While there are many search engines, digital marketers often focus on Google since it's a global leader in the search engine market.

In SEO, there's no consistent rule for ranking highly on search engines. Google and other search engines change their algorithm almost constantly, so it's impossible to make exact predictions. What you can do is closely monitor your page's performance and make adjustments to your strategy accordingly.

• Content marketing

As mentioned, the quality of your content is a key component of an optimized page. As a result, SEO is a major factor in content marketing, a strategy based on the distribution of relevant and valuable content to a target audience.

As in any marketing strategy, the goal of content marketing is to attract leads that ultimately convert into customers. But it does so differently than traditional advertising. Instead of enticing prospects with potential value from a product or service, it offers value for free in the form of written material, such as:

- Blog posts
- E-books
- Newsletters
- Video or audio transcripts
- Whitepapers
- Infographics

Content marketing matters, and there are plenty of stats to prove it:

- 84% of consumers expect companies to produce entertaining and helpful content experiences
- 62% of companies that have at least 5,000 employees produce content daily
- 92% of marketers believe that their company values content as an important asset

As effective as content marketing is, it can be tricky. Content marketing writers need to be able to rank highly in search engine results while also engaging people who will read the material, share it, and interact further with the brand. When the content is relevant, it can establish strong relationships throughout the pipeline.

To create effective content that's highly relevant and engaging, it's important to identify your audience. Who are you ultimately trying to reach with your content marketing efforts? Once you have a better grasp of your audience, you can determine the type of content you'll create. You can use many formats of content in your content marketing, including videos, blog posts, printable worksheets, and more.

Regardless of which content you create, it's a good idea to follow content marketing best practices. This means making content that's grammatically correct, free of errors, easy to understand, relevant, and interesting. Your content should also funnel readers to the next stage in the pipeline, whether that's a free consultation with a sales representative or a signup page.

• Social media marketing

Social media marketing means driving traffic and brand awareness by engaging people in discussion online. You can use social media marketing to highlight your brand, products, services, culture, and more. With billions of people spending their time engaging on social media platforms, focusing on social media marketing can be worthwhile.

The most popular digital platforms for social media marketing are Facebook, Twitter, and Instagram, with LinkedIn and YouTube not far behind. Ultimately, which social media platforms you use for your business depends on your goals and audience. For example, if you want to find new leads for your tech startup, targeting your audience on LinkedIn is a good idea since industry professionals are active on the platform. On the other hand, running social media ads on Instagram may be better for your brand if you run a B2C focused on younger consumers.

Because social media marketing involves active audience participation, it has become a popular way of getting attention. It's the most popular content medium for B2C digital marketers at 96%, and it's gaining ground in the B2B sphere as well. According to the Content Marketing Institute, 61% of B2B content marketers increased their use of social media this year.

Social media marketing offers built-in engagement metrics, which are extremely useful in helping you to understand how well you're reaching your audience. You get to decide which types of interactions mean the most to you, whether that means the number of shares, comments, or total clicks to your website.

Direct purchase may not even be a goal of your social media marketing strategy. Many brands use social media marketing to start dialogues with audiences rather than encourage them to spend money right away. This is especially common in brands that target older audiences or offer products and services not appropriate for impulse buys. It all depends on your company's social media marketing goals.

To create an effective social media marketing strategy, it's crucial to follow best practices. Here are a few of the most important social media marketing best practices:

- Craft high-quality and engaging content
- Reply to comments and questions in a professional manner
- Create a social media posting schedule
- Post at the right time
- Hire social media managers to support your marketing efforts
- Know your audience and which social media channels they're most active on

- ## Pay-per-click marketing

Pay-per-click, or PPC, is a form of digital marketing in which you pay a fee every time someone clicks on your digital ads. So, instead of paying a set amount to constantly run targeted ads on online channels, you only pay for the ads individuals interact with. How and when people see your ad is a bit more complicated.

One of the most common types of PPC is search engine advertising, and because Google is the most popular search engine, many businesses use Google Ads for this purpose. When a spot is available on a search engine results page, also known as a SERP, the engine fills the spot with what is essentially an instant auction. An algorithm prioritizes each available ad based on a number of factors, including:

- Ad quality
- Keyword relevance
- Landing page quality
- Bid amount

PPC ads are then placed at the top of search engine result pages based on the factors above whenever a person searches for a specific query.

Each PPC campaign has one or more target actions that viewers are meant to complete after clicking an ad. These actions are known as conversions, and they can be transactional or non-transactional. Making a purchase is a conversion, but so is a newsletter signup or a call made to your home office.

Whatever you choose as your target conversions, you can track them via your chosen digital marketing channels to see how your campaign is doing.

- ## Affiliate marketing

Affiliate marketing is a digital marketing tactic that lets someone make money by promoting another person's business. You could be either the promoter or the business who works with the promoter, but the process is the same in either case.

It works using a revenue sharing model. If you're the affiliate, you get a commission every time someone purchases the item that you promote. If you're the merchant, you pay the affiliate for every sale they help you make. Some affiliate marketers choose to review the products of just one company, perhaps on a blog or other third-party site. Others have relationships with multiple merchants.

Whether you want to be an affiliate or find one, the first step is to make a connection with the other party. You can use digital channels designed to connect affiliates with retailers, or you can start or join a single-retailer program. If you're a retailer and you choose to work directly with affiliates, there are many things you can do to make your program appealing to potential promoters. You'll need to provide those affiliates with the tools that they need to succeed. That includes incentives for great results as well as marketing tools and pre-made materials.

- ## Native advertising

Native advertising is digital marketing in disguise. Its goal is to blend in with its surrounding content so that it's less blatantly obvious as advertising. Native advertising was created in reaction to the cynicism of today's consumers toward ads. Knowing that the creator of an ad pays to run it, many consumers will conclude that the ad is biased and consequently ignore it. A native ad gets around this bias by offering information or entertainment before it gets to anything promotional, downplaying the "ad" aspect.

It's important to always label your native ads clearly. Use words like "promoted" or "sponsored." If those indicators are concealed, readers might end up spending significant time engaging with the content before they realize that it's advertising. When your consumers know exactly what they're getting, they'll feel better about your content and your brand. Native ads are meant to be less obtrusive than traditional ads, but they're not meant to be deceptive.

- **Influencer marketing**

Like affiliate marketing, influencer marketing relies on working with an influencer—an individual with a large following, such as a celebrity, industry expert, or content creator—in exchange for exposure. In many cases, these influencers will endorse your products or services to their followers on several social media channels.

Influencer marketing works well for B2B and B2C companies who want to reach new audiences. However, it's important to partner with reputable influencers since they're essentially representing your brand. The wrong influencer can tarnish the trust consumers have with your business.

- **Marketing automation**

Marketing automation uses software to power digital marketing campaigns, improving the efficiency and relevance of advertising. As a result, you can focus on creating the strategy behind your digital marketing efforts instead of cumbersome and time-consuming processes.

While marketing automation may seem like a luxury tool your business can do without, it can significantly improve the engagement between you and your audience.

According to statistics:

- 90% of US consumers find personalization either "very" or "somewhat" appealing
- 81% of consumers would like the brands they engage with to understand them better
- 77% of companies believe in the value of real-time personalization, yet 60% struggle with it

Marketing automation lets companies keep up with the expectation of personalization. It allows brands to:

1. Collect and analyze consumer information
2. Design targeted marketing campaigns
3. Send and post digital marketing messages at the right times to the right audiences

Many marketing automation tools use prospect engagement (or lack thereof) with a particular message to determine when and how to reach out next. This level of real-time customization means that you can effectively create an individualized marketing strategy for each customer without any additional time investment.

• Email marketing

The concept of email marketing is simple—you send a promotional message and hope that your prospect clicks on it. However, the execution is much more complex. First of all, you have to make sure that your emails are wanted. This means having an opt-in list that does the following:

- Individualizes the content, both in the body and in the subject line
- States clearly what kind of emails the subscriber will get
- An email signature that offers a clear unsubscribe option
- Integrates both transactional and promotional emails

You want your prospects to see your campaign as a valued service, not just as a promotional tool.

Email marketing is a proven, effective technique all on its own: 89% of surveyed professionals named it as their most effective lead generator.

It can be even better if you incorporate other digital marketing techniques such as marketing automation, which lets you segment and schedule your emails so that they meet your customer's needs more effectively.

If you're considering email marketing, here are a few tips that can help you craft great email marketing campaigns:

1. Segment your audience to send relevant campaigns to the right people
2. Ensure emails look good on mobile devices
3. Create a campaign schedule
4. Run A/B tests

- Mobile marketing

Mobile marketing is a digital marketing strategy that allows you to engage with your target audience on their mobile devices, such as smartphones and tablets. This can be via SMS and MMS messages, social media notifications, mobile app alerts, and more.

It's crucial to ensure that all content is optimized for mobile devices. According to the Pew Research Center, 85% of Americans own a smartphone, so your marketing efforts can go a long way when you create content for computer and mobile screens.

Creating a digital marketing strategy

For many small businesses and beginner digital marketers, getting started with digital marketing can be difficult. However, you can create an effective digital marketing strategy to increase brand awareness, engagement, and sales by using the following steps as your starting point.

a) Set SMART goals

Setting specific, measurable, achievable, relevant, and timely (SMART) goals is crucial for any marketing strategy. While there are many goals you may want to achieve, try to focus on the ones that will propel your strategy forward instead of causing it to remain stagnant.

b) Identify your audience

Before starting any marketing campaign, it's best to identify your target audience. Your target audience is the group of people you want your campaign to reach based on similar attributes, such as age, gender, demographic, or purchasing behavior. Having a good understanding of your target audience can help you determine which digital marketing channels to use and the information to include in your campaigns.

c) Create a budget

A budget ensures you're spending your money effectively towards your goals instead of overspending on digital marketing channels that may not provide the desired results. Consider your SMART goals and the digital channel you're planning to use to create a budget.

d) Select your digital marketing channels

From content marketing to PPC campaigns and more, there are many digital marketing channels you can use to your advantage. Which digital marketing channels you use often depends on your goals, audience, and budget.

e) Refine your marketing efforts

Make sure to analyze your campaign's data to identify what was done well and areas for improvement once the campaign is over. This allows you to create even better campaigns in the future. With the help of digital technologies and software, you can obtain this data in an easy-to-view dashboard. Mailchimp's digital marketing analytics reports will help you keep track of all your marketing campaigns in one centralized location.

Power of digital marketing

In the past, the marketing process was one of the most challenging processes among all. It is obviously required to market your product in one way or another. With no internet and very less technological advancement, the only way was to communicate from word of mouth or either from posters. Since the digital marketing came into existence, the marketing has been so easier you can simply share your content on a website online or make use of social media to let people know what you want. Advertising different kinds of technologies is a lot common as well.

How Has Digital Marketing Helped In This Era?

Digital marketing has helped this era in several ways. The brands can benefit their marketing by using it. It's not only about the advertisement, you can simply advertise as much as you would want through this, but along with that, you can simply provide your customers support 24/7 through the online portal. The use of this social media interaction with different marketing brands makes it easier for them to receive positive as well as negative feedback from their customers. Therefore, these types of interactions and working platforms have revolutionized the platform of different businesses and brands.

a) Easily Accessible

The access to word of mouth in the past times was a very difficult one when one person would have to deliver the message to the other. With digital marketing in the process, it became easier to access different people. All they had to do is to write up some SEO or web content and share it. On the other hand, Facebook, YouTube, and many such sites have helped in easily accessing the market. It has been encouraging for all the brands to easily access their customers to have the direct contact with them to manage and check the feedback daily.

b) Refining Strategy

In businesses, what's most important is the strategy you build. It is never necessarily true that the first strategy that you have planned will become successful, neither is it the other way around. Therefore, once you are done and planned your weekly or monthly budget and market value you simply put it on the web. Later in coming days, you can see how much has it worked? If you don't find it satisfying and working up to the mark, then that's simple you can see the pros and cons and refine your plan on that very spot rather than waiting for the whole week or month.

c) The Level Of Play Is Same Regardless Of The Brand

What can be meant by the level of play in the sales market is that there are always different brands in which some are expensive and have a greater budget? Therefore, they could pay more money and easily advertise more on the television or put big posters outside. All these costs much and easily implemented by only some high money raising brands. With digital marketing coming into existence all this wiped away, all the brands can be at same level of advertising through the social media and also by maintaining their official website.

d) Greater Exposure

With digital marketing, your businesses get a better exposure. In the old times, the work only expanded to the place where your people could spread the word. However, now after digital marketing, your work won't be staying still at a single place. Rather you will see it expanding from country to country until it reaches worldwide. Once you optimize the key word content on your website, then you can see a long-term investment.

e) Use A Reliable Digital Marketing Agency

For those running a business, it is impossible to run a digital marketing campaign alone. Thus, you should hire a professional agency that has the ability to deliver the best results.

Digital marketing is a simple way to enhance a business with investing less amount of money. It benefits us in a lot of ways, provide a greater engagement with many different companies and brands. Also, a lot of interaction with customers so to provide them with the best products. With this kind of marketing people get to choose for themselves either to join in or not so, it is not intrusive at all making the different viewers and customers happy and satisfied.

Chapter 2

Mind Set Development: Thinking like a digital marketer

Important characteristics to be successful Digital Marketer

It's no secret that success in the world of digital marketing requires a special kind of person because digital marketers need the skills, knowledge, and experience of a variety of different professionals. Digital marketing is a career that combines traditional marketing, web design, SEO, social media marketing, content writing, and much more, so the traits required to succeed are many and varied. Many of the traits of a successful digital marketer pertain to things like being independent and self-motivated to work and to learn, but it's also necessary that you be able to work as part of a team, lead others, and communicate effectively with clients, coworkers, and the public. Here are some of the other key traits you need to succeed in your digital marketing career.

- ## The Ability to Self-Start

Remember back in high school or university when you got paired with other students to work on projects, and you always dreaded being partnered with the ones who were notorious for not following through with their portion of the work? Well, those types of people would never succeed in digital marketing. Digital marketing is a field that often offers a great deal of professional freedom, so if you can keep yourself motivated and on track, then you'll find lots of doors opening for you in this business. For one thing, many digital marketers end up working for themselves or for a firm that grants them autonomy, so you alone will be responsible for managing your own time and projects. Unless you can keep yourself motivated, you'll find it difficult to stay on track with your work.

- ## Loving a Challenge

Because of things like ever-evolving technology, consumer habits that are always changing, and the increasing sophistication of both the internet and its users, the world of digital marketing is in a state constant of flux. There are always new things to learn, new arts to master, and new hurdles to overcome, and it's an absolute must that you love puzzles, tests, and all the other things that make life both interesting and challenging. Furthermore, every project in digital marketing is different, so you have to be willing to think on your feet, be creative, and be ready to look at things from a different perspective in order to achieve the goals your clients are trying to reach.

- ## Flexibility and Adaptability

Another consequence of digital marketing being ever-changing is that it requires digital marketers to be equally willing to change and adapt. Flexibility, therefore, is an essential quality in a digital marketing professional, because you always have to be prepared to adopt new practices, update your skill set and knowledge base, keep up with industry best practices, and stay current with the latest technologies and trends. A great example of how things are always changing in digital marketing is the Google algorithm. The algorithm is always being updated, and every time they release a new version, it changes the way digital marketers and SEO specialists approach their craft.

• A Passion for Learning

As you may have guessed, lifelong learning is an absolute must-have quality for anybody interested in digital marketing, because the field is always evolving, as is the technology that informs it. There are many ways you can keep up to date with the latest information, tech, and best practices, and they include:

- Attending conferences
- Building a strong network with other digital marketing professionals
- Keeping apprised of industry news, including when and what the latest algorithm changes are
- Taking refresher courses on important topics
- Learning new skills, like web design and creation, copywriting, and statistics
- Another reason the love of learning is so important is that it makes you curious, and that means you'll be more willing to take minor risks when it comes to pushing the envelope and testing new practices.

• The Desire to Help Grow Other Businesses

The main goal of digital marketing is to help businesses gain exposure, find new leads, build their brands, increase conversions and sales, and grow their companies. In today's world where people rely on the internet for things like researching products, choosing a business to deal with, and making purchasing decisions, it's integral that a company have an online presence if they want to succeed, and digital marketing professionals must have a passion for making this happen. Not only do you have to want to help other people grow their businesses, but you must also be dedicated to their success because their triumphs are also yours.

- ## Communication Skills

Digital marketing is all about communication: it's about disseminating messages, building relationships, and establishing trust, and none of this can be accomplished without excellent communication skills. The key here is being able to take a message and convey it to an audience in a way that's clear and concise, but also interesting and relevant. This requires being able to see things from another person's perspective, being able to communicate ideas in a way that will make sense to others, and having a knack for knowing what others will find entertaining and worthwhile.

- ## Leadership and Management Skills

Like most industries, digital marketing is a multifaceted field that requires many different skills and qualities. Because of this, digital marketing professionals often work in conjunction with others who have skills that complement their own, such as an SEO expert teaming up with a web designer and content marketer. As such, it's essential that you be able to lead and manage a team to make sure things get done properly and on time, and that often means delegating tasks, dividing projects, and making sure everybody stays focused and on track, all while keeping the client apprised of your progress. A related trait that digital marketers require, therefore, is the ability to collaborate and work well with others, because digital marketing is a team effort rather than a solo endeavor.

- ## Trustworthiness, Reliability, and Dedication

Similarly, because digital marketing requires you to work with both other professionals and clients, it's integral that your partners and clients be able to trust you. In order to gain that trust, you must be a hard-working, dedicated, and reliable person who goes the extra mile to get a job done, who can complete projects on time and according to plans, and who doesn't give up when things get tough. Project managers and coworkers need to know that when you get a project, it will come back perfect; clients need to know that when they trust you with their business, they're going to get their money's worth. Similarly, you must be dedicated to the pursuit of digital marketing excellence in general, and that means staying on top of the latest news and best practices so you can always offer top-notch services.

- **Strategic and Analytical Thinking**

The final trait of a successful digital marketer is the ability to think strategically. Like traditional marketing, digital marketing is about taking a goal and figuring out how to help a client achieve that, and this requires the ability to analyze situations, data, and opportunities to determine the best course of action. For instance, if a client wants to increase leads and conversions, it could be your job to evaluate their current efforts, see what's lacking and where, and come up with a comprehensive digital marketing campaign to produce the results the client is looking for.

Digital marketing doesn't require a great deal of specialized knowledge, but the key is that you have the traits necessary to make it in this competitive but highly rewarding field. Most of the technical knowledge and skills can be learned, but the traits and qualities that are required for success can't be acquired in the same way. Successful digital marketing professionals all tend to have a love for learning, are self-starting individuals who are driven and passionate about what they do, and who can work independently, lead others, and work well as part of a team. Finally, being a successful digital marketer means caring about the successes of others, because digital marketing wouldn't exist without the businesses who rely on you to help them grow and succeed.

Popular Digital Marketing Jargons to learn

According to Wikipedia Jargon is sometimes understood as a form of technical slang and then distinguished from the official terminology used in a particular field of activity. Another word to express Jargon is known as buzzword.

Digital marketing is an all-encompassing term for any type of online marketing that occurs through a digital device which is an internet-connected tool. Knowing the terms associated with the work helps to understand the actual process and progress in work by marketers.

Digital Marketing terms and definitions can be categorized under the various specific domains—SEO or search engine optimization, social media marketing, email marketing, video, paid advertising, influencer marketing, digital PR, and others. On the other hand, there are the general, technical, and operations-related terms that are relevant across the divisions.

Here is a list of the top 25 most critical digital marketing terms and what they mean. Knowing them will decipher the industry.

1. A/B Testing

Also known as split testing – the process of testing two versions of digital content with a target audience, the preference is learned by measuring by conversion rate – used in testing e-newsletters, email subject lines, social ads, calls-to-action, and landing page copy to know which version has the greater chance of giving the desired action such as subscribing for a paid membership.

2. Affiliate Marketing

A strategy which rewards 'affiliates,' i.e., people or organizations outside the business for bringing new customers or visitors; done through a promotion like ads or content on the affiliate's website for a commission based on the number of customers generated – used on personal or lifestyle sites for product recommendations.

3. Brand Positioning

Building a brand identity and connecting to it as different from competitors through tone, voice, and visual design of ads, promotion, logo, representation in social media, etc. – creates market differentiation, builds reputation, drives sales, and focuses your brand marketing message.

4. Content Strategy

Planning and implementation of digital content to make it work towards a uniform end; includes creating and distributing content for digital marketing campaigns such as blog posts, articles, social media posts, videos, podcasts, e-books, guides, webinars, etc.; includes testing to gauge content performance – content is the base on which all marketing techniques are built. This digital marketing term is a fundamental component of content marketing campaigns as well.

5. Conversion Rate

The percentage of users who completed the desired action; calculated by dividing the overall size of the audience with the total number of 'convert' users; for instance, those who clicked on an ad – conversion rate percentage is used as a metric upon which marketers try to improve further growth. Digital marketing strategies are almost always data-driven, and this digital marketing term is one of the most common parameters measured to determine the performance of any campaign.

6. CPA or Cost per Acquisition

A pricing model that charges only when leads, sales, or conversions are generated; it is a financial metric that measures the costs of acquiring one paying customer – it helps marketers to know how much a company can afford to pay for leads and drive new customer growth.

7. CPC or Cost per Click

A pricing model that measures the cost for each click on an ad; designed to drive traffic to a website – critical digital marketing metric showing how much a business pays for someone to click on their ad.

8. CPM or Cost per Thousand

A pricing model that measures the cost of an online ad per 1000 impressions, impression being whenever the ad is displayed on a web page – ideal for creating brand awareness and delivering a direct message on high-traffic websites.

9. CRM or Customer Relationship Management

A set of applications that marketing firms use to manage customer data, analyze customer interactions, and receive relevant data in real-time – CRM is used to update and improve customer relationship strategies, to personalize and target marketing services.

10. CTA or Call-to-Action

Referring to a piece of content, such as a text, banner, form, button, or image on a web page (or email) prompting visitors to perform a specific action; includes instructions or directives to either read more content, join, subscribe, sign up or buy – CTAs guide visitors in their buying journey, impacts conversion rates.

11. CTR or Click Through Rate

The percentage of users who click on links placed in emails, ads, websites, etc.; measures the users actively engaging with linked content on a site with the formula: CTR = (click-throughs/impressions) x 100 – this metric helps to understand customers and finetune target audience.

12. CRO or Conversion Rate Optimization

The process of optimizing a website to increase the percentage of visitors performing the desired CTA; a marketing system to raise the percentage of visitors converting into paying customers – CRO methods create a better user experience, generate quality leads, shorten time to close deals.

13. Email Filtering

A technique that organizes emails based on a word or phrase in an effort to keep the user's inbox free of spam – used to steer clear of spam filters and avoid blacklisting; allows targeted reach.

14. Engagement Rate

Metrics to track the involvement of the target market with a brand's content; understood as the number of likes, comments, and shares or interactions with videos, updates, blogs, etc. – important in social media marketing to measure success through brand visibility, affinity, and credibility. This digital marketing term is one of the strongest measures of social media campaign success, especially when the focus is to build a strong subscriber or follower base for your social profile.

15. The Funnel

The sales funnel displaying the buying process from a lead to a customer.

   a) ToFu or Top of the Funnel

The first stage of the buying process where visitors are still looking for information – this stage requires building trust through quality content to motivate visitors into the next stage.

    b) MoFu or Middle of the Funnel

The middle stage where buyers have identified their problem and need but continue research – here leads are transferred from marketing to sales.

    c) Bofu or Bottom of the Funnel

The last stage where the buyer is getting ready to buy after identifying several vendors – consultative approach to help a customer to come to a decision will seal the deal.

16. GTM or Go-to-Market strategy

Plan specifying how to present a product's unique value proposition to achieve a competitive advantage in reaching customers – provides a roadmap for launching a product to achieve product-market fit.

17. KPI or Key Performance Indicators

A metric or quantitative benchmark to track progress towards marketing goals; KPIs should be SMART or Specific, Measurable, Achievable, Relevant, Time-Bound – used in measuring performance and course correction.

18. Keyword Stuffing

The practice of using too many keywords in the content to improve visibility on search engines; harmful tactic attracting penalization by search engines – sifts bad marketing firms from the good ones who focus on keyword research to optimize web advertising and website search engine placement to match high traffic keywords.

19. Lead Generation

Educating visitors on product or service and the industry where visitors, in turn, provide qualitative information to the sales team – helps to capture qualified leads.

20. LTV or Lifetime Value

Also called CLV or Customer Lifetime Value – the best estimate of expected revenue from an average customer – is used to calculate the overall impact of one sale throughout the entire customer relationship.

21. Paid Ads

Generating website traffic through paid ads that ensure the marketing content will jump to the head of the line; include two main categories of social media ads and display ads that are targeted based on trackable behavior metrics – helps to reach relevant leads.

22. Relevancy Score and Quality Score

To decide how relevant an advertisement is and how it compares to other similar ads on the platform; higher scores mean more ads will be shown over competitors – improving these scores help to lower CPC.

23. ROAS or Return on Ad Spend

Marketing metric to measure the efficacy of advertising campaigns and calculate the return on investment for paid marketing such as spending on ads – ROAS helps to evaluate which methods are working and how to improve future advertising efforts.

24. SEM or Search Engine Marketing

Strategies to get higher placement on search engines by bidding on search terms and increase the visibility of a website in search engine results pages; refers almost exclusively to paid search advertising and alternately referred to as pay per click or PPC – used to generate better leads.

25. Target Audience

The ideal client persona in mind while strategizing new ad campaigns or content; the group of people who could benefit from a company's offers – determining a target audience through paid and organic efforts helps to increase sales and grow the reach.

Chapter 3
Freelancing as a Digital Marketer

What is Freelancing?

Freelancing is a type of self-employment. Instead of being employed by a company, freelancers tend to work as self-employed, delivering their services on a contract or project basis. Companies of all types and sizes can hire freelancers to complete a project or a task, but freelancers are responsible for paying their own taxes, health insurance, pension and other personal contributions. Since they work for themselves, freelancers must also cover their own holiday costs and sick pay. At the same time, self-employed professionals can set their own working hours and make working arrangements that fit their lifestyle – either working remotely or from their clients' offices.

There are many different types of freelancers, but they tend to be knowledge workers who possess a high-level of skills and knowledge in a certain area, such as designers, writers, programmers, translators, project managers and so on.

There is, however, another group of self-employed professionals that often get classed as 'gig workers' or 'contractors.' Self-employed handymen, cleaners, construction workers and drivers would fall into this category. The most distinct difference between freelancers and gig workers is that the former tend to rely on the internet to deliver their work..

What are the advantages of being a freelancer?

With the number of freelancers on the rise year on year, many describe the decision to go freelance as life-changing. Here are a few of the commonly touted advantages to quitting the standard 9-to-5 job and becoming a freelancer.

a) Flexibility to decide how, when and where to work

One of the biggest perks of being your own boss is that you don't have to ask anyone's permission to work from home, start late or work while you travel. You decide your own business hours and you choose where to work from. If that means taking Wednesdays off to visit your grandma or working late into the night and sleeping until noon – so be it!

b) Choosing your own clients

Once your business is running smoothly, you'll also have the freedom of choosing the clients you actually want to work with. And that's a wonderful feeling! Whenever you feel like you don't mesh with the client's personality, don't like someone's attitude or payment terms, you can shift your energy to finding a new gig instead of fighting constant battles with the client.

c) Keeping all the profits

One of the best things about working as a freelancer is that you can see a direct link between working hard and your account balance. Since you keep all the after-tax profits, it is also up to you to decide how you want to allocate and spend the money.

Famous Freelancing Websites to Find Work

- Upwork.com
- Fiverr.
- Toptal.
- Jooble.
- Freelancer.com.
- Flexjobs.
- SimplyHired.
- Guru.
- Designhill
- LinkedIn and LinkedIn ProFinder
- We Work Remotely
- Behance
- SimplyHired
- Dribbble
- PeoplePerHour
- AngelList Talent
- DesignCrowd
- 99designs
- Working Not Working
- Webflow Experts
- YunoJuno
- Authentic Jobs
- TaskRabbit
- Flexjobs
- SolidGigs

Digital Marketing for freelancers

What do you get when you put together two of the decade's biggest buzzwords?

'Freelance' + 'Digital Marketing'…

An exciting new industry with an abundance of untapped career potential.

Why Become A Freelance Marketer In The First Place?

Businesses are spending bucket loads of cash on digital marketing. There's a TON of opportunity for freelance digital marketing specialists to grab their piece of the pie. Money being spent on online marketing is increasing - faster than the normal growth rate of other industries. This means by becoming a freelance digital marketer, you're going where the demand is and positioning yourself in a fast growing industry with a ton of opportunity for career growth and financial growth.

What Is Freelance Digital Marketing?

Freelance digital marketing refers to someone (the freelancer) offering a service(s) that helps a company to market its brand, product or service - online.

But for now, here's a quick outline of the 6 most common types of digital marketing:

1. **Paid Advertising**: Paying to display an ad on a platform. Examples include: Facebook ads, Google Ads, Quora and Reddit ads, Amazon PPC (Pay-Per-Click) ads and Google AdSense
2. **Social Media Marketing:** Utilizing social platforms to organically reach new customers and nurture existing fans. Examples are Instagram and Pinterest accounts.
3. **Content Marketing:** Creating valuable content in a way that draws search traffic and adds value to a brand, website or chosen platform (YouTube, Instagram etc.). This can be done through blog posts, videos, images, or any other form of 'content'.
4. **SEO (Search Engine Optimization):** Optimizing content, websites and/or other platforms to increase the chances of showing up at the top of a search result page from a search engine (e.g. Google) query.

5. **Conversion Marketing:** Usually conversion marketing focuses on lead generation (i.e. email list building) and product sales. Conversion marketers specialize in creating landing pages, opt-in forms, sales pages, email marketing campaigns and webinars.
6. **Affiliate and Influencer Marketing:** Refers to putting a reward system in place for those who refer or recommend a certain brand or product. Affiliates usually get a percentage of the sale, while influencers usually get a once off-payment or free product.

Within these different types of marketing, there are different experts and specialists. Digital marketing freelancers can specialize in any number of fields within those broad marketing categories.

Examples of digital marketing specialties are:
1. **Copywriters:** Persuasive writing specialists that craft text (also referred to as 'copy') to get readers to carry out a desired action or conversion goal.
2. **Paid Ads Experts:** Paid advertising campaign experts that usually specialize on crafting & monitoring ads for specific platforms (e.g. Facebook ads, Google Adwords, Amazon Ads, etc.).
3. **Affiliate Marketing Managers:** Experts that manage affiliate marketing programs for brands, products or services. These managers focus on signing up new and influential affiliate partners who have large audiences, handling current affiliates and keeping them happy, as well as managing the platforms that track affiliate sales and pay out affiliate commissions.
4. Email Marketing Specialists: Email marketing specialists that create email campaigns and sales funnels. The campaigns are focused around a series of persuasive emails designed to achieve a specific conversion goal, usually a product purchase.

Digital marketing Skills for non-Technical freelancers

1. **Community Management:** Managing a community is managing a group of people with common interest. Being a community manager will require you to post content on behalf of company.

1. **Posting Skills**: includes posting on different social media platforms, making schedule posts
2. **Advertising skills:** Advertising products or services on different platforms using different tools
3. **Acquisitions:** Selling skills
4. **Performance Measurement:** whatever you do as a digital marketer you need to be able to measure your performance.
5. **Client Dealing:** Client Dealing jobs include the ways to communicate with customers, getting their feed back and using that feedback to improve performances.
6. **Blog Creation:** Blog sites are those informally managed websites that talk about similar ideas or contents. Blog creation is very easy writing work that nin technical people can do.

Should You Become a Freelance Digital Marketer?

So let's review what we've covered so far, and see if becoming a freelance digital marketer makes sense for you:

- Digital marketing is a growing industry
- There's an abundance of opportunity

But is this career the right move for you?

Let's take a look at some of the benefits and downsides of a freelance digital marketing business.

The Benefits of Freelance Digital Marketing

With the low barrier for entry, it's easy to get started as a freelance digital marketer, and comes with some awesome benefits.

1. You can start a freelance career with little to no experience.
2. No capital is required; you can get started as long as you have a working laptop to deliver your digital products with.
3. One of the biggest benefits of this field - often cited by freelancers - is the ability to work from home or from anywhere in the world.
4. Another often cited benefit of freelancing is being able to set your own rates and choose how you get paid. Common freelance payment structures include hourly rates, retainer fees, payment on deliverable or revenue sharing.
5. Flexibility in who you work with also comes with another massive benefit: the ability to have a variety of clients lets you work on multiple projects and decreases your reliance on one employer or income stream.
6. Freelancers that successfully manage multiple clients (more on that in the scaling chapter) and multiple revenue sources are able to decrease financial risk.
7. Being a freelancer is essentially being your own boss, so suits entrepreneurial types well, and they often mention this as one of the greatest benefits of freelancing. You run the show. You get to decide your business culture, principles, working hours, and even who you work with.

The Downsides of Being a Freelance Digital Marketer

Along with the benefits of freelancing, there's also some very real downsides that should be taken into account before starting your digital marketing career.

1. Creating stable month-to-month income that's reliable can be difficult and leads to income insecurity. It can often be difficult to scale your freelancing business to multiple clients, and having only one client or project you're working on puts you at financial risk.
2. Since you're basically a business owner, you're ultimately the one responsible for everything. Everything is on your shoulders. No boss to tell you what to do, no company to absorb any mistakes. It's all on you.
3. That means you're also on the hook for managing everything on the financial side, including taxes, benefits, health insurance, and other necessities.

However, many of the downsides to working as a freelance marketer can be avoided with the right planning and execution.

Digital marketing tools to help you grow as a freelancer

If you are a digital marketer looking to boost your marketing strategies and ROI, you will want to know about certain tools that can make things easier. With digital marketing tools, you will be able to execute proper strategies in the right manner. These tools are designed to keep things organized, allowing you to make necessary customizations whenever needed.

After facing the previous challenges, we have to focus on creating better and more innovative strategies in future. Here we introduce ten most influential and creative digital marketing tools you should experiment with and try if you want to grow as digital marketer.

Top 10 Best Digital Marketing Tools

1. MailChimp
2. Google Analytics
3. Google Ads
4. Canva
5. Trello
6. Slack
7. Yoast SEO
8. Survey Anyplace
9. Ahrefs
10. SEMRUSH

1. MailChimp

MailChimp is a social advertising and email marketing tool designed to orchestrate and automate digital marketing campaigns. It is one of the best digital marketing tools you can get to improve your campaigns and track the traffic generated. Moreover, the platform allows multiple integrations with different SaaS companies. The tool is quite efficient for email campaigns, using which you can engage with your audience. MailChimp is a well-renowned name in the world of email marketing.

The features of MailChimp:

- Creates better content with easy-to-use design tools
- Use Ai-powered assistant for generating custom designs.
- Create personalized emails and get up to 6 times more orders using marketing automation
- Provides tools for getting insights and analytics at one place
- Also, provide a free plan for small marketers.

MailChimp incorporates pre-built, customizable email automation that makes it easy for you to reach the right audience at the right moment. The best part is that you can keep your brand top of mind and delight your customers with happy birthday messages, welcome automation, and order notifications.

Online retail and e-commerce businesses can significantly benefit from MailChimp, as it can help you drive traffic, increase conversions, and grow sales.

2. Google Analytics

Google Analytics is a powerful digital marketing tool that can help you with numerous marketing decisions. You can easily track your e-commerce business as well as goals that can help keep your company on track. Using the innumerable data insights that Google Analytics provides, it is easy for marketers to understand the directions required to take with the website modifications and changes. All you have to do is install Google Analytics on your site, and you are ready to go.

The features of Google Analytics:

- Provides you with information about traffic on your website that is divided by devices, products, pages, and more.
- Let you create your metrics, dimensions, and dashboard for easy access to data and information.
- Helps you understand your target audience in a better way. You will get real-time updates about your website's customers, including the pages they are currently exploring. This can help you make your landing page more engaging by providing the customers with a more intuitive experience.
- Let you uncover insights about how the business is performing.
- Let you share the insights with the help of various reporting tools.
- Let you organize and visualize the data suiting business requirements.
- Last but not least, Google Analytics comes with tons of features, functionalities, the ability to create customized reports and dashboard.

3. Google Ads

Google Ads can work for almost any business; it doesn't matter whether it is small, medium, or large. While many marketers think that Google Ads is too expensive, it is one of the most powerful digital marketing tools that can help your business reach new heights.

The features of Google Ads:

- Drive website visits
- Increase the call calls from customers through a click-to-call button
- Increase footfall in your shops

People need to learn Google Ads first in order to use it effectively; else you will be wasting your money (Learn to create Google ads here). The best part about Google Ads is that return on investment (ROI) is relatively easy to measure. Moreover, new artificial intelligence features make the platform a lot faster and easier to use. The AI features can help you get results faster in Display advertising.

The multiple targeting options allow you to target your customer base based on different factors like age, gender, location, profession, etc. This is something that you will not find in other digital marketing tools.

Most importantly, you can access Google Agency Account Strategist, where you can learn about the latest features that Google provides. Moreover, access to this means access to some beta testing as well.

4. Canva Business

If you are in digital marketing, you will understand the need for a quality design tool that can help you create impressive social media posts and other things in marketing. Canva is a prominent design tool that allows you to develop effective marketing campaigns through visual content that can be shared on your blogs, websites, social networks, and other platforms. Visual content is the backbone of any digital marketing campaign. In order to entice the targeted customer base, you need to design compelling posts.

The features of Canva:

- Canva allows you to edit posts and create graphs or any type and kind.
- The tool incorporates numerous templates. It boasts a massive library of stock images, photos, designs, icons, and vectors that you can use to create any type of visual content for your marketing campaign.
- It allows you to choose from a massive collection of designs, such as postcard, brochure, CD cover, wallpaper, book cover, resume, certificate, magazine cover, letterhead, presentation graphic, blog banner, card, poster, flyer, presentation, logo, and social media.
- Its simple drag-and-drop design allows you to create visual pieces according to your campaign. The best part is that you don't need an experienced designer to create visual content for your digital marketing campaign. It is so simple that anyone with no design background can use it.

5. Trello

If you are looking for a content management tool that will help you brainstorm and strategize content for your digital marketing campaign, you can opt for Trello. It is one of the most popular content management tools used by hundreds and thousands of digital marketers worldwide to create, schedule, and organise content online.

The platform keeps the whole team together, making communication a lot easier and manageable. You can assign multiple members from your team to a single card so that they can work on a project together. This way, you will know who's in charge of designing, writing, editing, posting, and adding call-to-action offers to a post.

The features of Trello:

- Allows you to create cards and incorporate notes on the card topic while creating deadlines and assigning topics to specific teams.
- Facilitates remote working where your teams can access their tasks and projects from anywhere. Also Read: How to increase productivity while working from home?
- You can use Trello for organizing your digital marketing campaigns and ensure that you never miss out on anything that your team is doing.

6. Slack

Digital marketers use Slack every single day. With Slack, you can discuss client work, new articles, new projects, new support tickets, share useful content and send messages.

If you have a distinct team of digital marketers, you will need a powerful medium to make effective communication with them. This is where Slack comes into play.

The features of Slack:

- Makes it easier to communicate with team members over the web in real-time.
- Let you follow everything related to the projects, teams and channels.
- Let you do message and video conferencing too.
- Assist the teams in collaborating from anywhere

While it seems like a messaging app, it does a lot more than that. Slack can potentially tighten up your organizational efficiency. It is not a collaboration or a project management tool. It serves as a messaging platform with a rich collection of options and settings. It lets you have group conversations that are searchable and public, including private conversations. You can change the color scheme of the interface and create different groups.

7. Yoast SEO

You probably have heard of Yoast SEO. It is one of the most talked-about and used WordPress plugins that help digital marketers to optimize their websites to perform better in search results.

Yoast SEO helps with the SEO details where WordPress cannot do much: for submitting sitemaps, managing keywords, creating content, and using webmaster tools, among other aspects.

The features of Yoast SEO:

- The tool comes with a plethora of features that helps in optimizing your website for search engines and make it easier to rank.
- Incorporates built-in content analysis, description management, meta keywords, rich snippets, social features, XML sitemaps, as well as features to manage duplicate content.
- Allows you to write better content for your digital marketing campaigns. The plugin provides you access to the Yoast SEO meta box to add meta description and meta title for your content. Moreover, you don't have to install a third-party plugin for XML sitemaps.
- It automatically produces XML sitemaps for websites and submits them to search engines.
- The best part, you can protect your RSS feed from plagiarism and content scrapers. This protects you from other websites copying your content and publishing it as theirs.

8. Survey Anyplace

SurveyAnyplace is the best tool for marketing professionals to create fun and interactive quizzes, assessments, and surveys for their targeted customer base. It is a great digital marketing tool that will enable you to engage with your target audience and help build brand identity and personality.

If you are bored of traditional surveys to know the current demand for a product or business, you can use this tool to implement some quality surveys for your digital marketing campaigns that will help you in the long run.

The features of SurveyAnyplace:

- Allows you to create questionnaires which return valuable insights
- Provides personalized advice in return to the respondents
- Helps in understanding the market demands, what customers want, what features are they looking for, and more.

With SurveyAnyplace, you can reflect your branding on questionnaires and surveys and build your own brand. In simple terms, based on the user experience, you can create your own brand that stands up to your customers' expectations. The best part is that the platform allows you to formulate your own questions, and you can include images as well in your surveys.

The surveys you provide are well-designed, simple, and compatible with mobile devices.

9. Ahrefs

Ahrefs offer a suite of search engine optimization tools, making it easier for you to optimize your website based on your marketing requirements. It is primarily used for checking backlinks, and with its massive data index, the tool is definitely one of the most sought after digital marketing tools in the market.

The features of Ahrefs:

- Let you optimize your website.
- Let you find the right websites for your content and strategically choose content topics.
- Helps in analyzing the competitors
- It is a comprehensive SaaS tool that offers snippets of testimonials, data index, and a free trial as well.
- Let you manage your projects.
- Let you track your ranking progress.

10. SEMRUSH

SEMRUSH is an all-in-one marketing toolkit that helps grow the online visibility of the business with SEO, content marketing, market research, advertising, social media management and search engine reputation management.

The features of SEMRUSH:

- Helps in boosting organic traffic with the SEO tools and workflow
- Assist in creating the content which ranks
- Unveils competitors' strategies and tactics
- Helps you discover the ways of reaching more prospects with less spending
- Supports in building social media strategies.

As per their official website, 7 million marketing professionals like to use SEMRUSH as their digital marketing tool. The tool has won many awards as the best SEO software. The tool is very easy to use where you just have to search out your keyword strategies, apply them and start tracking them. The tool is free for trial, but the user has to opt for paid plans after seven days.

With these tools, you will be able to better understand and manage your digital marketing campaigns. However, you need to know that while some of them offer a free trial, they are all paid. But, it is worth the investment.

Chapter: 4
Becoming a Successful Freelance Digital Marketer

Freelance digital marketer

Freelance digital marketers provide their services to companies, typically small-scale businesses or startups. Freelance digital marketing encompasses a variety of services such as:

- Content creation
- Social media marketing
- Building and managing websites
- Creating and running digital ads and campaigns

- Design services such as graphic design, User Interface/User Experience (UI/UX) design, or video production
- Hosting webinars or running podcasts
- Creating a 360-degree marketing or brand strategy
- Email marketing and campaigns
- Marketing research and analytics

A digital marketing freelancer is any digital marketer who runs their own business to help clients. The category is broad, so it can cover all types of marketing that are common today. Digital marketers often wear many hats, and some of their most common activities include:

- Writing copy for blogs, web pages, and social media
- Building websites and helping with design
- Managing social media accounts and communities
- Creating advertisements, including copy and visuals
- Designing visuals such as infographics
- Creating and editing videos
- Holding webinars or running podcasts
- Running ad campaigns and managing ad budgets
- Developing a campaign and marketing strategy for your clients
- Emailing your client's customers and managing email marketing campaign
- Generating leads and qualifying them
- Onboarding new clients and managing client meetings

The day-to-day work of any given digital marketing freelancers can be completely different. Some freelance digital marketing professionals and digital media consultants focus on creating brand strategies. Others might work with in-house teams to create ads that are part of those campaigns.

Most digital marketers work with clients daily and communicate regularly. Some may specialize in niche areas—such as writing and market research—where interactions are only a few times a week.

What are the pros and cons of freelance digital marketing?

Freelance digital marketers and professionals have many choices and specific areas of expertise they can pursue within their line of work. This abundance of options means you can have a wide range of experiences if you decide to become a digital marketer. It's smart to consider the pros and cons of joining this field as an independent professional.

Here are the ones most freelance marketers we spoke to share with us.

Pros

1. The ability to work from anywhere and travel or change locations at any time. While COVID has made work-from-home temporary for some marketers, freelancers always have this option thanks to the nature of digital technologies.
2. You can choose the work you want. Job services like Upwork provide you with access to many different digital marketing clients with their own needs. You pick the type of jobs, industries, and companies that you'd like to work with.
3. Work the hours you want as long as you hit deadlines.
4. Use the equipment and tools you have and prefer.
5. You can rely on other freelancers as needed for help or expertise, enabling you to learn as you complete your jobs.
6. You can receive more immediate payments when you use services that provide escrow.
7. You can work with clients anywhere. This gives you access to major markets and large corporations outside of the area where you live, potentially enabling you to charge higher rates for your work.

Cons

1. You're also running your own business, so there are tax filings, licenses, and other things you might need.

2. Invoicing, client management, social, and your own advertising still need to happen, but you can't bill these hours.
3. You only get paid for what you do. Sick days or weeks with few projects will mean that your revenue fluctuates.
4. Paid time off, insurance, and other benefits must be paid for entirely by you.
5. Some find the ongoing hunt for clients stressful.
6. Being a freelancer can be a challenge. Thankfully, there are many opportunities to partner with others in your community. Local and online groups, forums tied to job boards, and national organizations can all help you find other freelancers who might be able to answer your questions, make business suggestions, or otherwise help you to tackle the challenges that you face.

How much do freelance digital marketers make?

Remember that large and diverse list of skills you saw earlier? This range of skills within the career means that freelance digital marketers can earn entirely differently. According to ZipRecruiter, these independent professionals in the U.S. have annual revenues of between $22,500 and $127,000. The national average is roughly $69,000 per year or about $33 per hour.

The more specialized you are, the more you can charge for your services. Focusing on high-impact areas, such as managing large campaigns for enterprises or learning AI tools to create marketing analytics, can also help.

On Upwork, you can quickly find freelance digital marketers at vastly different pricing. Entry-level marketers tend to charge around $20 to $30 hourly. People with more experience and expertise can make up to $80 per hour. Top professionals often charge as much as $125 or $150 per hour, with some even charging upwards of $300 per hour for specific projects such as creating ClickFunnels campaigns from scratch.

What are the different digital marketing jobs you can do?

While there are many skills and tasks required of digital marketers, a quick look at available jobs shows a concentration in a few areas. So, let's look at five of the hottest areas for today's freelancers.

1) Facebook and Instagram ads

Facebook owns Instagram, so advertising on both channels can be managed through a single account in Facebook's Ads Manager. Many small businesses advertise and find customers solely via social media, making expertise here a big draw. Small and mid-sized businesses often need freelancers more than a full-time employee, so mastering ad campaigns on these platforms can help you work with a diverse range of companies.

2) SEO consulting

Search engines drive significant traffic for businesses, and that means they also drive sales. SEO (search engine optimization) work takes place on a website and follows current best practices to help that site's pages perform better for user searches. Organic ranking, as opposed to paid ads, can help any business.

3) Chatbots and customer service

Chatbots are a growing customer service tool because they can now easily integrate with websites and even Facebook accounts. You may have chatted with someone through Facebook Messenger that was actually a chatbot. Business owners often need help with these tools, from installation and creating answers to optimizing them for sales. New professionals can find a lot of work with platforms such as ManyChat.

4) Sales funnels and landing pages

Digital marketers must master the art of the online sale. In most cases, that means reaching out to the customer repeatedly and creating website pages designed to give visitors what they need to make a purchase. The overall process of interacting with people and getting them to buy through ads, emails, and website content is called a sales funnel. Landing pages are specific pages people arrive at that are designed to close the deal. Marketers create both of these for businesses to help them thrive.

5) PPC and Google Ads

Pay-per-click advertising is a type of ad model where you place ads with sites, especially search engines, and pay the publisher when someone clicks on the ad. PPC campaigns can either cost a flat rate or require you to bid around keywords. The most prominent PPC network is Google Ads. It's simple to run and works across nearly all ad campaign tools, making it one of the more common tools for marketers who create and run search ad campaigns.

A quick note is that Google's advertising program was initially named AdWords in 2000. Even though it shifted to the "Google Ads" branding 2018, many customers will still ask for AdWords help.

How to get started as a digital marketing freelancer

The demand for digital marketers is high and freelancing can be a smart entry point, but you need to do the challenging work of pitching your services to companies. On the bright side, you don't need to interact with HR and go through rounds of interviews, you just need to communicate with a team manager who is looking for specific help. There are some common steps you can take to start the process and make yourself a desirable option to companies.

Here are the seven things to know and do so you can get started as a freelance digital marketer.

1. Take a course to study what's new

There are many digital marketing courses available. Some come from small digital marketers and freelancers themselves while others are provided by universities and top marketing agencies.

Look for classes that can teach you about many different options and that show when they've last updated their materials. Information from just a few years ago may already be out of date and not relevant to you. If you take a course on a specific product, for instance, you need to be taught the latest version so you can understand how it works.

Certifications from well-known groups can go a long way in having a client trust that you can do the job they need.

2. Determine your skills

After you study and learn about the many different possible tasks within digital marketing, try them out. Your coursework may give you an overview of skills. If so, run through tests and programs to see where you excel. If not, create your own tests. Thankfully, there are many free tools for things like social media management, and most ad platforms will give you a small amount of free credit to try their system.

Through tests, trials, and asking colleagues and teachers to look at what you've created, see where you did well. Create a list of the skills that others praised. Now, create a separate list of the tasks and skills that you enjoyed. When a certain skill overlaps both categories, highlight it and add it to a new list of the services you can offer.

3. Pick your specializations

The new list will show you where you can succeed, because digital marketing requires both technical knowledge and a passion for the work. Focusing on areas you enjoy and have sufficient skill can turn freelancing into a long-term career that you enjoy. It keeps all of the "pros" we mentioned earlier available to you and minimizes the stress that the "cons" will place on you.

Specializing also minimizes your work. You'll find a few skills to practice and know to narrow your search for work around these items. When companies interview you, you'll know what to focus on and demonstrate. This focus prevents you from having to try and learn it all, or from looking for jobs that aren't a good fit.

4. Find expert help for ongoing support

Freelancers often can't get on-the-job training or ask a manager. However, you can find many mentors online. Groups on LinkedIn that focus on digital marketing, forums, Reddit, and local community businesses often are willing to help beginners learn the ropes and avoid mistakes. Start to create a community of people who do similar work to you so you have people to ask. It can make a world of difference when a client asks for something new or if a specific tool isn't working for a job.

Freelancers should also look for mentors who know about running a business. You'll likely face questions about how to approach clients, manage time, pay taxes, and more that are specific to where you live and work. A broad community can help you find the right answer or put you in touch with a professional who can address the issue and keep your business in good standing.

5. Follow blogs that focus on your specialty

Digital marketing practices change regularly. There's always a new platform update or social media channel ready to be tapped into. Search engines change how they rank websites, and certain ads become too familiar to be successful. The way you consume media is likely different now compared to five years ago, and so is all the marketing around that media.
The experts in the field address this by doing two things: They create blogs and they follow other professional blogs about their specialty. Blogs have become areas to showcase expertise and discuss the latest trends. Reading blogs regularly can help you stay on top of changes and discover new opportunities.

You'll also find research that impacts how you advertise. For instance, a few top blogs compiled data toward the end of 2020 that showed, despite the ongoing pandemic, people are searching for more specific businesses and products "near me" than ever before.

6. Create your profile

Once your brain is full, it's time to start putting that knowledge to use. Create your freelance portfolio and profile to show who you are and what you offer. Tell a story around your skills and highlight work you've done. If you haven't landed that first job, use things created for school and online courses, or build something from scratch to demonstrate your capabilities.

Using services like Upwork can make this process easier because you've got a specific portfolio template to follow. You can also look at other marketers to see how they explain skills and offers. You'll see what works and what you don't like. Plus, you can browse jobs at the same time and ensure that your profile mentions the skills and software you see as being the most sought after by clients.

7. Start applying for entry-level jobs

After the skills are honed, you have ongoing lesson plans set up, and a profile ready, it's time to start applying for jobs. Use job boards, LinkedIn, and word of mouth to let people know you're offering digital marketing services. Seek out companies creating job posts and apply to them. Respond to requests with information, samples, and personal notes. Don't use a standard reply for everyone!

You'll want to customize every pitch and response. It builds trust and helps people understand you better. It may take a few attempts, but you'll soon find the perfect place to start your new career.

How to Become a Freelance Digital Marketer Pro?

Here's a step-by-step approach that will help you learn how to become a freelance digital marketer:

Step 1: Choose Your Marketing Specialties

Digital marketing is an umbrella term that includes various kinds of marketing efforts requiring a battery of varied skills. Focus on a few skills that deeply align with your natural abilities or experience. This will help you enjoy your work better. For example, people who are naturally good at language and communication will do well in providing services such as content writing and social media marketing. On the other hand, if you have worked with organic content or search for a substantial amount of time, you can choose to focus on services such as Search Engine Optimization (SEO) and Search Engine Marketing (SEM).

Step 2: Build Your Brand

In the digital world, branding is everything. You want to know how to become a freelance digital marketer? You have to build a personal brand. Clients typically work with freelancers they already know or get introduced to via their references. Hence, you must make your work known to your network. You can also post regularly on professional networking platforms such as LinkedIn. Furthermore, creating assets, such as a website and a digital portfolio, will be beneficial to increase your visibility.

Step 3: Legally Register Your Brand

Though it is not mandatory to register your business at the initial stages, you should aim to do it as soon as possible. The advantages of registering your brand or company are brand and logo retention, eligibility for funding opportunities, and better credibility.

Step 4: Level up Your Business and Entrepreneurship Skills

As with any other business, you need more than your core skills to become a successful freelance digital marketer. For example, even if you are a great writer or a very successful social media marketer, you need good business acumen to keep your business running in the long term. So try to acquire and hone essential business skills such as skills in communication, presentation, analytical ability, and financial literacy.

Step 5: Establish a System for Creating Proposals

A digital marketing proposal should typically contain two main types of information: logistical information and a pitch.

The logistical information will include items such as the types of services, project timelines, resource information, and other such points. The pitch will contain pointers addressing the 'whys' and 'hows' of your association. First, decide on a few headers that must go into any proposal and then customize further depending on the client's specific requirements. Make your work easier by using templates.

Step 6: Set Your Pricing Strategy

Successful freelance digital marketers know how to price their services well. However, in the initial phase of your career, you might not have many benchmarks to decide on your pricing strategy. One of the easiest ways to develop a pricing strategy is to network with others in the same profession and do some secondary research. If you are unsure how to set a price for your services, you can start by calculating the time you will need to do a specific job. Then decide on a minimum hourly rate and assign the requisite value to your service.

Step 7: Join Freelance Platforms Such as Fiverr and Upwork

If you are thinking seriously about how to become a freelance digital marketer, you must acquit yourself with online platforms such as Fiverr and Upwork. These are marketplace platforms that connect freelance digital marketers to potential clients. Getting clients, however, depends on how well you build your profile and the pricing of your services. Don't get demotivated if you don't get clients immediately. Most newbie freelancers get their initial clients through their immediate network before finding work through these platforms.

Step 8: Promote Your Freelance Work Availability on LinkedIn

LinkedIn offers a creator mode that allows you to publish your profile, skills and services. Utilize the feature to its fullest and regularly post relevant updates about your digital marketing services.

Step 9: Connect With Other Freelancers for Advice

Networking with other freelancers will help you understand the nuances of the digital marketing field and increase your visibility. You can find freelancers working in your niche on LinkedIn and connect with them or follow them to stay up to date with their activity. In addition, you can pick their best practices and incorporate them into your promotional strategy.

Step 10: Build a Loyal Customer Base

Wondering how to become a freelance digital marketer who gets paid handsomely? The high-paying clients for digital marketing professionals will always come via references. So, ensure that you create fans out of your existing client base. You can also proactively ask your clients to provide testimonials on LinkedIn.

Step 11: Organize Your Time

Many freelance digital marketers are good at their jobs but struggle with deadlines and managing multiple clients because they don't optimize for time. Avoid going all out while working on projects, as this style of working leads to burnout in the long-term and is not sustainable. Instead, use calendars and project management tools to keep track of your time. Working hard can equal working smart.

Step 12: Monitor Cash Flow

In most cases, digital marketing agencies and freelancers cannot get payments in advance unless you're running ads. Therefore, you need to maintain financial discipline to keep your business running smoothly. Ensure that you clearly state all payment terms in your agreements, raise invoices on time, and receive complete and timely payments, which might require some follow-ups on your end.

Chapter 5:
Freelance Operations

How To Manage Your Freelance Business

The world of digital marketing is an exciting and expansive one. It moves quickly, and businesses that use it well see an incredible return on their investment.

It's also an industry very friendly to freelancers. Whether you're an experienced marketer considering stepping away from your in-house employee position or looking to pivot into something new entirely, freelance digital marketing is an attractive option to those with the right creative skills.

Once you start bringing on clients, everything changes. You're now essentially operating as a business, and a critical factor to your success will be how you manage your time. You want to be smart about your day-to-day operations because any improvements to your output can make a big impact on your profits.

What Does a Freelance Digital Marketer Do Every Day?

If you're considering a career in digital marketing but aren't sure what the job entails, it can be helpful to understand what a freelance digital marketer does on a day-to-day basis:

- Reply to emails and set agendas
- Monitor progress on various tasks at hand and make a to-do list.
- Executing the task list
- Set up meetings with existing and potential clients to share progress and receive new briefs
- Raise invoices and manage other financial matters

Digital marketing is an exciting field to join. Whether you are just exploring it or considering it a full-time career, you won't regret it. But don't just jump in headfirst. It takes time to develop expertise, and the best way to do that is by having your basics right.

Create the Perfect Freelancer Daily Routine

Creating a routine around your business will help you to streamline operating times, deliverables, and get into a flow with each client so you can give them your best work. This will also help you manage your personal life and your time by essentially setting office hours for yourself so you're not constantly working around the clock.

Just like your last place of employment, or any other business, how you manage your time will ultimately contribute to your success. Flexible working hours is one of the huge lures of freelancing, but it can also be the downfall of the ill-prepared.

So here are top 6 tips for creating the perfect schedule.

1. Create a schedule and stick to it

This is the best advice anyone can give, and the hardest to follow. Create a schedule...then actually stick to it. As a freelancer, there's very little built-in structure to your day (as opposed to a traditional workplace), so you have to be the one to create that structure. If you have a lot going on and a ton of interruptions throughout the day, this can be incredibly hard to pull off, but if you get this right, it can be a lifesaver.

Creating a time management plan will help you get more done, keep your commitments (and clients), and give you the freedom to plan ahead for things like vacations, time off, sick days, etc.

- Tip # 1 - Know Your Commitments

Unfortunately, freelancers don't have the same protections that a regular job might have, and a single mistake can get you fired. Knowing your personal and professional commitments will help you map out a strategy and schedule for getting your work done and getting your deliverables handed off on time.

You can use a project management system, your calendar, or use a spreadsheet or document to keep a running list of your commitments easily available, but whatever you choose, make sure to regularly jot down all your deliverables and commitments with clients and your home life so you can stay on top of everything.

- Tip # 2 - Communicate With Your Clients

Communication and transparency might be the most important factors for any successful relationship, and it's no different for the freelancer and client relationship.

How about this for a nightmare scenario:

You neglected to tell your only client about an upcoming vacation where you will be completely unreachable... (exploring the depths of the Amazon, maybe?)

While you're away, the websites you've built for your client go down, and you're the only one with access and the know-how required to fix the problem. Because you've never had a problem with your client sites going down before, you neglected to prepare for any problems.

You come back home refreshed from your trip and check your email: "You're Fired!!!"

Turns out your client lost a ton of money while their sites were down and they had no way to contact you and fix the issue.

Now this may be an extreme example, but it illustrates the point: communication is key to your success. Would you take a vacation from your regular 9-to-5 without informing your boss in advance? No, and while your freelance clients are not your "boss", the same principle applies to keep all parties happy.

Setting expectations and being up front in advance with your clients about your schedule protects you from misunderstandings arising from poor communications.

- **Tip # 3 - Create Office Hours for Each Client**

Your time is the most precious asset you have in life and work. You can't get it back once it's gone — and that's why it's so important to protect your schedule and make sure it's working for you. You don't want to get in a situation where it's open season on your schedule. Random meetings and phone calls in the middle of a project can derail your work and throw off your entire week. Setting specific office hours for each client will help you to plan out your week and also help them manage their own schedule.

You can use an automated appointment setting tool like Calendly to give your clients scheduling abilities with your calendar You can connect Calendly to your calendar and specify which times you want to be publicly available for scheduling, then give your client a link that lets them schedule a time directly on your calendar that works for you both.

- **Tip # 4 - Have a Freelance Morning Routine**

One of the best ways to avoid this common problem and keep yourself in the productivity zone more often is by establishing a personalized morning routine for yourself. There's been a ton written on morning routines across the internet, so we're not going to cover specifics in this article. Instead we want to briefly mention this practice as a potential tactic to help you get your day under control. Having a morning routine that includes things like time for exercise, planning, reading, or meditation, can anchor your day and set your mindset for productivity.

- Tip # 5 - Experiment With Productivity Hacks

It's worth exploring some of productivity hacks for yourself to see if one fits well with your schedule and helps you become more productive. What works for some people might not work for you, so that's why it's important to experiment with different strategies and find the right fit for your working style and schedule.

- Tip # 6 - Eliminate Distractions

In today's world we're under constant bombardment from pings, notifications, calls, and all manner of distractions. Each one feels urgent, but in reality most aren't. Finding a way to eliminate distractions during your work day will help you get more focused work done.

A simple trick you can do to help boost your productivity immediately is to place your phone in the other room or put it into airplane mode during a focused work session.

2. Create Dedicated Office Space at Home

Setting aside dedicated office space and treating your home office like a workplace is a great way to psychologically trick yourself into feeling like you're at work, thereby creating an environment that's more conducive to focused work, and kick starting productivity when you're in your home office.

The best way to accomplish this is to set aside specific space in your home as an office. Ideally, if you have an extra room, make that your new workspace. Or if space in your home is more limited, you can create a work-specific corner of a room to function as your new office.

Similar to the advice above, creating work/life separation by renting an office or co-working space or even spending a chunk of your day at a coffee shop has helped many freelancers be more productive. And because freelancing can be a lonely business sometimes, an added bonus to finding a public working space is being around people. Isolation can be a real problem for many freelancers and having daily opportunities to interact with people can have a positive impact on your health and wellbeing. But whether you spend time at coffee shops or get a co-working space or office to work from, make sure it fits with your budget and the space isn't too distracting.

3. Dress for Work Like You're Going to the Office

Getting dressed like you're going to work can be a way to psychologically trick yourself into work mode. The ritual of getting ready in the morning and dressing like a professional can kick start your mind into getting ready for the working day, and can also have positive effects on your mood.

In one study on the impact of workplace attire on self-perceptions, "respondents felt most authoritative, trustworthy, and competent when wearing formal business attire but friendliest when wearing casual or business casual attire."

Kate King from MsCareerGirl.com says:

"I'm not saying that you should glean your confidence from your clothes. But dressing professionally even for a freelance task—where no one is observing you—may help you treat this work more seriously. It can also boost performance if you are struggling to stay on task."

This advice might not apply to everyone, but for the ritual-minded folks out there, this single trick could help you manage your freelance business.

Time Management Tips for Freelancers

Managing your time can be hard as a freelancer, but it can also be critical to your business. If you're billing by the hour, managing your time and reporting back your hours to your client may even be a contractual obligation. That's why getting good at this skill early on in your freelance business will serve you well later on. So here we will be covering awesome ways to manage your time as a freelancer, including ways to create processes, ways to outsource work and automation tips.

Let's dive right into our top time management tips for freelancers.

• Create Processes

Creating processes that you can repeat over and over again is one of the best ways you can save time as a freelancer. A process is nothing more than a repeatable and communicable set of tasks that you need to execute in order to get the job done. Turning your core tasks into processes and documenting them will allow you to easily replicate the series of tasks necessary to get the job done, and make it much easier to outsource your work to a virtual assistant or subcontractor.

That's why one of our top recommendations is to create processes and record those processes via screen sharing app or simply by writing them down on a document and refining those processes as you go. By refining and optimizing those processes you're making them better and better over time and helping you save more and more time.

One of the keys here is to identify tasks that you tend to repeat over and over again - once you do that, you can start building processes around them that help you scale that task. By creating processes in your business you're on the way to turning your freelance side hustle into a streamlined operation.

- ## Outsourcing

By outsourcing tasks that could easily be done by another freelancer or virtual assistant, you're freeing up precious time for you to run your freelancing business, get new clients, and make your business more efficient. Any repetitive task that takes up your time, can be given to another freelancer at a more competitive rate, and can easily be documented and turned into a process, is a good candidate for outsourcing.

However, outsourcing work as a freelancer is tricky business. You run the risk of hiring people who don't know how to get the job done, exhibit communication and time zone issues, and actually inject more chaos and confusion into your business then you already had. But getting outsourcing right can be a huge benefit as you grow your business.

- ## Recurring Billing

Setting up recurring billing for your clients is an awesome way to automate away a core piece of your business. Getting paid is the lifeblood of your business, and finding ways to eliminate friction around the payment process for you and your clients can be a game changer. Tons of tools and apps let you create recurring invoices, store credit cards and charge your clients on a schedule as well as help you maintain records for taxes.

Common Freelance Mistakes to Avoid

Freelancing has a lot of ups and downs. Since you're essentially running your own business, there are a lot of things that can go wrong especially if you're new to this and have no prior experience freelancing or managing clients.

A lot of new Freelancers make big mistakes early on in their careers, which can lead to a project falling apart, unhappy clients, and ultimately the end of their freelancing career. Pay attention to following list of mistakes, as any one of these mistakes could be a project-killer.

Freelance Mistake #1 - Scope Creep: The Silent Killer

This term "scope creep" gets thrown around a lot but there's a lot of misunderstanding about what it actually is. Scope creep simply means that the scope (AKA the overall requirements of a project), has got out of control and that ultimately the project has become undeliverable. If you find that unforeseen deliverables are piling up and time spent on a project is getting out of control, you're the victim of scope creep.

This can easily happen if a project Scope of Work (SOW) is not clearly defined. If you don't have a clearly defined SOW, too many changes and uncontrolled client requests can result in the project getting out of control. Once that happens, all your profit can vanish, too, as you spend more and more time on the project trying to get it back on track.

How to Avoid Scope Creep as a Freelancer?

- Know your project, commitments, and client - having a broad understanding of the project and all its moving parts will help you plan ahead and avoid scope creep.
- Create a detailed SOW (Scope of Work) with clearly defined deliverables, deadlines, and contingencies.
- Have a plan in place for change requests and communicate your policy in advance. From time to time your client may request changes or additional tasks (added scope) while you're working on their project. If you've notified them in advance of your policy with changes/added scope, there won't be any surprises when you bill the client for the changes.

Freelance Mistake #2 - Having Only One Client

The danger of having one client should be obvious. If that client leaves or the project comes to an end, you're back to zero and you've got to hustle for your next client. Contractors don't have the same protections in place as full time employees and most contracts can be terminated without notice. Don't get too comfortable with only one client, even if that one client is a full time gig. In fact, I'd argue that taking a full time client can put you at a massive disadvantage because it makes it hard to grow your business by winning new clients. Having multiple clients protects you from losing all your revenue if one leaves.

How to Avoid the One Client Freelance Trap?

- Choose projects that don't eat up all your time so you can layer on additional clients.
- Go after high paying projects with higher profit potential.
- Outsource, automate, and delegate - if you're doing everything yourself, you're at risk of burning out and spending all your time on a single project, so find ways to extend yourself by minimizing your personal time spent.

Freelance Mistake #3 - Picking the Wrong Clients

Similar to the above, this huge mistake can put your business at immediate risk. Choosing the wrong clients to partner with can spell certain doom for your new freelance career.

You should avoid:

- Clients that don't pay
- Clients that expect the world from you for nothing
- Clients that don't understand the value of your services
- Clients that don't communicate and give you what you need to get the job done...
- There's a million reasons a client might not be a great fit for you, but working with the wrong clients can turn into a time and resource black hole.

How to Avoid Picking the Wrong Freelance Clients

- Do your research - know the client in advance of a working arrangement. Do they have a history of paying on time? Do they have reviews on freelance websites? Do your due diligence for peace of mind?
- Get to know the client before working with them. In your initial discovery calls with the client, try to feel out who they are as a potential client. Do their expectations seem unreasonable? Do they have a solid understanding of your services and the value you bring to the table?
- Do an initial limited-scope project with the client to feel out the working relationship and if it's right for you before a big commitment project.

Chapter 6
Finding, Negotiating and Managing clients

How to find and communicate with your clients

Communication is your core skill when it comes to looking for clients and ensuring jobs are a success. Digital marketing requires constant work with clients to understand their business and audience, especially when you're new. You'll want to learn about people, create personas, discover the best channels and times to do outreach, and learn who your clients see as their most profitable customers. This requires you to talk, ask questions, and listen.

One of the best places to do this is on the system that manages your tasks and contracts. While you can communicate via email and things like Slack, messages can often get buried and it becomes easy to miss deadlines, changes, or other contractual requirements. Start with a platform that keeps it all in one place, creating simple areas for finding clients, finalizing contracts, messaging, and updating milestones. Upwork and others put these all in one place, while still making them easy to search.

Make it easy on yourself by starting on these platforms. Heading over to a freelance job page and then using that same site for everything else will help you avoid confusion or missed communications as you begin your career. There are also built-in opportunities for feedback, making it one of the best tools for digital beginners.

Negotiation Skills

Digital marketers who have attended the best negotiation classes can leverage their training to create win-win solutions with their clients.

If you are a digital marketer, here are eight powerful reasons why you need to master negotiation skills.

1. To claim value

Have you ever heard the phrase "giving away the farm?" Digital marketers often find themselves giving away too much value while gaining too little in exchange. If your clients or customers insist on getting concessions during negotiations, apply the process of logrolling to ask for concessions in return. Simply put, use the "if/then" negotiation phrase. For instance, "if I complete your project by your preferred date, would you be willing to pay commissions on your new service we're able to bring to market early?"

To truly master claiming value in negotiations, digital marketers should avoid limiting themselves to binary choices of 'Yes' or 'No'. A negotiations course can equip marketers to have options beyond what has been offered.

Delivering premium value to your client in your negotiation meetings requires preparation. Research your client's market and their company. Write out your questions. You'll be more likely to impress your client by coming across as more professional, well prepared, and able to demonstrate your prior experience in delivering results in the client's industry.

While most clients in a vertical market may want similar services and results, the differences in each client's ranking of their priorities can account for the vastly different winning client proposals and presentations produced by the top digital agencies. So ferret out your client's top priorities. It's your mission to figure out each client's ranking to understand their trade-offs, even if your client hasn't ranked their priorities.

2. To offer the best value

Enduring business relationships are built upon a foundation of negotiations based on value creation and value exchange. In order to come up with a win-win solution between you and your digital marketing client, it's important not just to focus on claiming value, but to also create reciprocal value.

Win-win value exchange is where you reach a digital marketing settlement that can't be improved by further negotiation. Negotiation classes can help digital marketers learn how to explore and pursue creative options that exploit opportunities for value creation and exchange.

For instance, if your prospective client posted an advert for email marketing services, you can use proven negotiation strategies to upsell for extra services. You could end up creating more value offering pay-per-click (PPC), newsletters, or social media marketing to improve the client's performance of the advertised email marketing service. Showcase your worth to prospective clients by having an updated service portfolio, offering timely customer support, and documenting your proven return on investment (ROI).

3. To form strategic partnerships

Whether you're running social media campaigns, sending out email newsletters, working with influencers, or managing SEO, you likely need to partner up with other professionals and clients. Use your negotiation training to identify partners with shared vision and principles, and to achieve mutually beneficial agreements.

With the right partners, you can communicate terms that allow each partner to:

- Build individual and collective brands
- Widen audiences
- Expand customer bases
- Share marketing resources

- Boost revenue growth
- Access additional talents

While some partnerships may be for temporary and short-term campaigns, some of the most profitable partnerships might evolve into long-term unions, such as joint ventures. Negotiate win-win terms to ensure successful partnerships that bring satisfaction and drive up win rates and profits.

4. To hire the best talent

As a digital marketer, you may often find yourself looking for fresh talent to deliver on client briefs. You may want to hire a permanent employee, engage a freelancer, or take on an intern. Whatever the case, you want to bring on board a talented professional at the right price and level of commitment.

Hiring the best talent typically involves negotiating. Many negotiation classes offer employers simulation scenarios on how to handle employee recruitment, interviews, and salary negotiations. Work out and agree on the best terms that encourage the employee or freelancer to provide their best output. It's worth exploring what your new employee values most. Will your new joiner value being able to choose their hours and being able to work from home? If so, then perhaps you can offer a lower rate of pay. All too often hirers dream of their most ideal working arrangement and end up paying top dollar for their inflexibility.

Offer your new talents corresponding pay and perks that may translate to better marketing campaigns without worrying about your staff being poached by other players. Use your negotiation skills to lock in and motivate great talent and put your expectations in writing.

5. To attract lucrative offers

Almost every business in the world needs some form of marketing. If your marketing campaigns have shown a track record of successful and consistent results, then you rightfully deserve more requests from your existing happy clients and new prospective clients.

As a marketer, you probably know that your client results are only good if others know about your clients' successes. Use your negotiation skills to communicate your past successes and expectations. Presenting this information effectively should increase your win rates and decrease your time to closure with new clients. While marketers are usually skilled at marketing their own and their clients' services, negotiation classes should translate your unique selling points into tradeable higher margin wins.

Some negotiation essentials you can use to pursue and attract lucrative digital marketing contracts include:

- Be thoroughly prepared to discuss your prior results, and be transparent.
- Ask former and current clients for written recommendations and testimonials.
- Set rates that reflect the services your client will need in order to deliver on their goals.
- Give yourself some room to retreat on your rates and know which services are a must-have versus non-essential for each client.
- Apply market segmentation, such as offering different packages for different groups.
- To streamline resource allocation
- The allocation of marketing resources has a significant impact on different levels of a business. You have to decide what marketing mix elements to invest in, which team roles to assign, and what platforms to use for your campaigns.

As a digital marketer, you may have to negotiate with your client on where to place resources. For instance, will a Pay Per Click (PPC) and remarketing strategy complement the SEO component or will blogging work better to attract, engage, and retain your target audiences?

Use your negotiation skills and business savvy to prioritize across expenditures. Negotiate to attract additional or premium funds to maximize the quality and effectiveness of your marketing campaigns.

6. To outperform the competition

It used to be that startups and small businesses could not aspire to compete against big corporations and multinationals. However, with online platforms for digital marketing, even small businesses can claim market share when competing against the big guns.

If you're a competent marketer, you most likely want to increase your clients' sales or products' market share. Knowing how to negotiate prepares you to position yourself and your clients against big and small competitors alike. Taking a negotiation class can help you communicate your unique selling proposition better to highly engage your target market.

7. To improve marketing services

Being a master of negotiations involves a lot of listening. When you pay keen attention to what your clients are saying, what the client's customers are saying, and what the market, in general, is saying, then you find opportunities to improve and better focus your digital marketing services.

For instance, when different clients keep asking for more or better content, then you know it's time to invest more in your content creation and premium content quality. If clients are asking for more automation, then maybe it's time you invested in chatbots.

You may go into a contract negotiation thinking your client requires one service. However, by paying close attention to what your client is saying, you might identify previously undisclosed pain points, and discover unexplored opportunities which could result in higher pay for your business.

Client Retention - How To Keep Your Freelance Clients Happy

By now you should know your niche and some strategies for getting freelance clients, and hopefully you've got a client or two already signed and working with you. Which leads us to the next big step in your freelance marketing career:

Learning how to keep your clients happy and getting them to stick around, AKA, retention.

Why Freelance Client Retention Is So Important

When you first start out as a freelancer, it's a bit like learning how to swim for the first time. You jump in the water, flail about, sink a few times, and eventually you either learn how to stay above water or you get out and give up.

Starting out as a freelancer is like that.

Sink or swim.

New freelancers are all over the place:

- Trying everything they can to get new clients
- Trying new tactics and learning new skills
- Winning and losing clients
- Figuring it all out on the fly...

But eventually you will reach a tipping point where you need to streamline your day to day operations if you're going to continue to grow. And that's where client retention comes in. Retention is such a critical component to your freelance success that we decided to dedicate an entire chapter of the guide to getting it right.

So what is freelance client retention and why does it matter so much?

"Retention simply means keeping your clients around (retaining them) so that they continue to work with you and continue to pay you."

As defined by Thrive Themes

If your clients aren't renewing their contracts or are walking away from your campaigns, that means you have to constantly go out and get new clients to stay in business. Alternatively, retaining current clients takes a lot less work and is more cost effective than constantly chasing after new clients. Getting a new client requires hours of work, possibly an advertising budget, and a ton of effort to onboard them, whereas keeping a current client happy is far less laborious.

In fact, for companies, according to huify.com, it may be up to 5 times more expensive to acquire a new customer versus the costs of retaining current customers, and while this guide is for freelancers, not traditional companies, we believe this is just as important if not more so for the average freelancer who relies on 1 - 5 clients.

Fix Retention Before Bringing on More Clients

You wouldn't continue trying to fill up a leaky bucket if it has holes in it would you?

If you haven't fixed retention problems before trying to grow, you'll find yourself trying to fill up the proverbial leaky bucket. As clients leave, you will be forced to constantly go out and acquire new clients to fill your revenue gaps and that is ultimately much more expensive than it is to keep your current clients.

After working with a client for a while, building your relationship with them, and getting results for their campaign, it becomes much easier to continue that progress than it does to start over from scratch with a new client. Many freelancers don't consider the impact that client retention has on their business because they may be in hustle mode trying everything they can to bring on new clients.

"People are willing to pay more if they know they're going to get a good experience. With good experiences come greater margins and also greater customer retention." - Brian Solis

So how can you change your mindset and start serving your clients better?

One approach is to start treating your freelance jobs like a business, instead of a side hustle. It's a simple mindset shift, but one with massive upside potential.

Freelancing Business VS Freelancing Side Hustle

Treating your freelance activities like a business instead of a side hustle might be the power move you need to grow your profits and eventually, one day, turn those activities into a real business.

What does it mean to treat freelancing like a business and why is it so important to your success?

As a freelancer it's easy to get into the trap of thinking of yourself as simply a contractor... as somebody who does side work for people, but the reality is you are operating as a business whether you think of it as one or not. You have to deal with some of the same issues businesses face every day: Taxes, profit-and-loss, revenues, getting clients, losing clients, customer service...

And every one of those functions can make or break a freelancer's career.

Businesses operate as a structure designed to generate profit, and streamlining necessary functions is one of the ways they achieve that goal... and there's no reason a freelancer can't do the same thing.

In order to do that, however, you have to approach your freelancing activities as a business and start looking for ways to streamline your operations.

1. Relationship Building

In a very real sense, a freelancing career - just like a business - is nothing more than a collection of relationships and agreements. You form a relationship, agree on an exchange of value, and then have to deliver on that agreement.

It doesn't matter if you're selling a one-time product or ongoing services, as a freelancer your relationship with your clients will determine your long-term success. If a business operates with honesty and integrity, and creates value in the marketplace, they have the chance to build great relationships and generate goodwill and repeat business with their customers as well as referrals.

The same is also true for freelancers.

Building strong relationships for the freelancer is crucial. Without great relationships built on trust and value, your clients will leave and you will be forced to constantly search for new clients. Once a relationship has soured, you're also at risk of receiving negative reviews from a client, putting future client acquisition in jeopardy. That's why we consider relationship building so critical to client retention and your long term freelancing success.

2. Create a Mission Statement

A mission statement is a written statement (usually no more than a couple paragraphs) that businesses often create in order to codify a specific set of values to use internally and as a way to communicate those values to their ideal customers. This is also a great way for a freelancer to start building a "business mindset", and set rules for how they're going to work with clients (relationship building).

But why should you bother? As a freelancer, you have a lot going on, right?

The reason is simple: a mission statement is a simple, powerful way to communicate to your clients and contractors what you're all about and how you can add value to their businesses and lives.

If, for example, you find yourself struggling to explain why you're a great fit for a client's business, then a mission statement might be just the thing you need to gain clarity the value you can bring to the table.

Below we're going to walk through a brief exercise for creating a mission statement for your freelance digital marketing business.

On a sheet of paper write down brief answers to the questions below:

1) Who does your business serve? (Note: for this question, you want to write down your ideal client.)
2) What value do you deliver for your ideal client?
3) What is your ultimate goal for your business?
4) What are your core values, strengths, and promises that you can give your ideal market?
5) What do you do better than anybody else in your field?

Now you have a simple framework that you can use to create your own mission statement. A typical mission statement is only a few sentences maybe at most a couple paragraphs. It's actually pretty difficult to condense all that down into a few sentences, but once you have it the way you want it, it can be a powerful device for client acquisition and for building your "business mindset."

Here's an example from Lindsay Pietroluongo on the Elegant Themes Blog:

"I provide tailored ideas, polished articles and trustworthy editorial support for creative brands and professionals. Elevated writing endures, and I work to create the type of warm, unforgettable copy that's always charmed me." - Lindsay Pietroluongo

Here's a few tips for writing your freelance mission statement:

- Keep it short, impactful, and powerful.
- Consider your long term strategy - don't create a mission statement that limits your growth, and be ready to adapt it on the fly if needed.
- Write with your ideal clients in mind, speak to their needs and problems.
- Treat it as an evolving document. Go back to it often - as your business and skill sets change, so too might your mission statement.
- Share it with friends, family, employees, contractors, and your clients for feedback.

Now that you have your mission statement ready, you can use that on your website, proposals, and any other assets you have to help you better earn and retain the right clients.

3. Have a Friction-free Client Intake Process

Eliminating friction during the client intake process can have a huge impact on your relationships with new clients. It's all about positive first impressions. The harder you make it for a client to do something like sign an agreement with you, send you payment, or continue on as your client, the more you increase the likelihood that they will drop off simply due to frustration.

The following principle should be used throughout your operations:

- Streamline everything that you possibly can and
- make everything super easy for your clients and contractors.
- Think about it from the perspective of your client.

Let's say you've got an awesome new client on the hook. They're super excited to sign up with you! Sweet! Unfortunately, you have an insanely difficult onboarding process and everything starts to slow down: your contracts look like a team of corporate lawyers drafted them, your proposal isn't clear (prompting a ton of back and forth), and you only accept paper checks via snail mail.

Pretty soon your new client is starting to lose interest with all the back and forth, and once that happens the relationship is already on the fence.

- **Customer Service = Customer Happiness**

Now that you're starting to think about your freelance work like a business, the next big area to tackle is customer service. If you're like most freelancers, your clients are paying you for your expertise and results. They contracted with you to help them grow their organization, and they may be paying you a lot of money, in which case they're probably looking at their relationship with you as an investment. Which is why customer service and customer happiness being so important to retention.

Once you start to see your clients as customers, and use some basic principles of customer service to keep them happy, your relationship will begin to improve as well. Getting customer service right is fairly simple in theory but often hard in practice. Keeping your clients in the loop, responding to their emails, texts, and calls, being on the ball with your contracts, and helping them when needed are all key pillars of an awesome freelance customer service strategy. By contrast, if you're managing your projects on the fly and your communication is erratic, your client might start to feel like you're dropping the ball, and that could factor in when it comes time to evaluate your relationship.

Try creating simple rules and processes like the following for yourself to stay on top of client happiness:

1) Depending on the project needs, send a report to your client every day, once a week, or twice a month as a way to manage the scope of work.
2) Set a recurring calendar item once a week to hold a client update call.
3) Create a rule for yourself and your contractors that you never wait longer than 1 hour to respond to a client request.

Whatever processes you decide on to keep clients happy, write them down and make sure you stick to them.

- **Create a Plan To Deal With Negative Customer Feedback**

Now that you're thinking about your customers and clients in a new light, It's time to prepare yourself for the inevitable negative pushback, review, or complaint. As you grow you're bound to ruffle a few feathers, make mistakes, or miss the ball on a campaign or two. That's why it helps to have a plan in place for negative feedback, and we've got you covered with the LATTE approach.

The LATTE approach to negative customer feedback:

LATTE is an acronym that stands for:

L. Listen to your customer's complaints

A. Acknowledge the problems

T. Thank the customer for communicating and letting you know about it

T. Treat the problem

E. Explain how you treat the problem

These simple rules can help you stay on good footing with your client.

Nobody likes a hothead, so to turn the situation around, deal with the problem head-on, with grace, and with the goal of turning lemons into lemonade (sour into sweet).

How to Keep the Scope of Your Project in Check?

The single most important thing in your relationship with clients will be your project Scope of Work (S.O.W.) and contract.

The super simple "Project Management Triangle" concept illustrates the need for a well-managed project, and makes the case that quality work for any project is determined by three main factors: budget, deadlines, and scope:

If you accurately plan out the scope, time it will take to complete (including deadlines), and the cost of projects, you should be able to create quality results and avoid problems like Scope Creep.

FreelancerMap.com identifies Scope Creep as one of the top reasons freelancer projects fail:

"One of the biggest things to keep in mind for projects is that they change. Ideas, priorities and goals evolve. If these changes are not handled properly, the so-called scope creep can occur. When a project's scope keeps growing or changing without control mechanisms in place, things tend to get out of hand."

If your project snowballs out of control and you're unable to meet your obligations, your awesome new freelance gig will soon be a thing of the past. Having a reasonable and manageable Scope of Work to follow is one of the best ways to protect yourself. If you can actually hit your deadlines and fulfill your obligations, you'll be in great shape with your client.

Managing Client Expectations (Promise Low, Deliver High)

Is it possible to have happy clients by doing less work? Yes!

But how is that possible?

It comes down to setting appropriate expectations for your working relationship in advance of starting a project in order to maintain fluid operations for the duration of the project. That helps you keep your client happy and your project on task. In fact, setting appropriate expectations is absolutely key to a successful relationship.

You don't want to enter into a contract with open-ended deliverables and expectations that are too high because eventually you will fail to meet your obligations to your client, they will become dissatisfied, and the working relationship will sour.

By setting manageable expectations for your project that you can actually deliver on (and hopefully over-deliver on), you're benefiting yourself and your client. And, the best part of promising low and delivering high means less work for you and happier clients.

Here are four tips for setting appropriate expectations in your Scope of Work, initial client calls, and contract:

Managing Client Expectations - Tip # 1

Know exactly what you can deliver within a reasonable time frame and make sure that each action item is clearly written down in the deliverable portion of the contract or scope of work. Make sure your client understands that adding extra items (added scope) mid-campaign is not included, must be agreed upon, and will add additional charges to your next invoice.

Why's it so important? Leaving yourself open to randomly added scope will hurt your chances of delivering on your promises, eat away at your profits, and eventually hurt your client relationship.

Managing Client Expectations - Tip # 2

Make sure your client is fully on board with all the deliverables and understands everything in the SOW. Even if you have to go through each portion together, make sure you're both on the same page so there's no confusion down the road. Why's it so important? Transparency and communication are key to developing a healthy relationship with your client. If they know what they're buying, there won't be confusion down the road.

Managing Client Expectations - Tip # 3

Clearly outline all dependencies and client deliverables that must take place in order for you to complete your work. If you're upfront about everything you need to get started, there won't be any surprises for the client. If the client doesn't understand that they need to get you certain items in order for you to proceed, you'll be left hanging and potentially upside down on your contract.

Freelance contract client deliverables example

Section 2, Client Deliverables

1. All images, graphics, fonts, and logos to be used in creation of branded profiles, blog, etc.
2. Provide consultant with possible regular (weekly or bi-weekly) meeting times during business hours (Monday - Friday / 8am - 5pm). Travel time is part of the consultants scope as long as it's within regular business hours and does not interfere with the work-plan deliverables schedule (Monday - Friday / 8am - 5pm), however, travel expenses are to be reimbursed by client.
3. Provide consultant with initial discovery meeting during week 1 of Phase 1 in order to determine all assets to be made available to consultant as well as ongoing or next-step client deliverables. (It's best if this takes place in the first day or two of week 1).
4. Provide consultant with all necessary materials to perform target market research, market analysis, product research, etc. Dependency: This is required by the end of the first week of Phase 1 / Consultant will provide a list of materials needed during the discovery meeting.
5. Log-in access to all servers and systems. Dependency: This is required by the end of the first week of Phase 1

Why's it so important? As you get to work, there's a ton of things you might need to complete your deliverables: client software passwords, design specs, content assets... the list goes on and on. Prepare for that in advance so your work progresses smoothly.

Managing Client Expectations - Tip # 4

Don't promise results that you can't deliver. If you're unsure of the actual results you can deliver, then use language in your contract that makes it clear you are not guaranteeing anything. Why's it so important? There's no faster way to sour a relationship with a paying client than to under-deliver on results. If you set expectations of dollar-value results, your client will expect that, and if you can't meet your promises, your new client relationship will be on the rocks.

Equally as important as setting the correct expectations in your Scope of Work is creating a contract that accurately reflects the SOW. So before you get that signature, make sure your contract is airtight and you're confident in what you're agreeing to.

How to Send Deliverables to Your Clients

A deliverable is nothing more than a task or an item that you agree to deliver to your client as part of your Scope of Work and contract. It could be as simple as a graphic (like an icon or logo), or it could be more complex (like a series of blog posts). Whatever it is, make sure you have a process in place to actually get those over to your client. Think about deliverables as the lifeblood of your contract and your relationship with any client. By staying on top of those deliverables and getting them in on time per your agreements, you're paving the way for a great working relationship. So set a predetermined schedule for turning in your deliverables — that you can actually meet — and communicate that in advance with your client so they know what to expect.

Actually sending in those deliverables could be done in a variety of ways: you might send them over email or a secure system like Dropbox, or simply notify the client that the task is done over SMS (if the job doesn't require sending any files). Another common way freelancers manage their projects is to get their clients connected up in a project management system so they can view the tasks that you're working on in relation to the actual project.

Follow Up with Your Clients

A simple way to keep your clients happy is to update them as you progress. You can do this by sending project updates, feedback, results, reporting dashboards, or whatever makes sense for your project. Communication is the key. Check in with clients daily, weekly, or on whatever recurring schedule works for you and them. This will go a long way to supercharge your relationship with that client over time.

But be warned: once you set this in motion, make sure to keep it in motion. That's because once your client gets used to regular project updates, they won't take kindly to uncommunicated changes in the schedule.

This goes back to setting appropriate expectations:

Only commit to deliverables you can actually meet. If you agreed to an hour meeting every single day, you might eventually find it hard to meet that requirement.

Meet Project Deadlines

Deadlines are common to many freelance projects. You might be working on the launch of a new product or working with a sales team that has quarterly targets to hit. So it goes without saying that meeting project deadlines is going to be a huge factor in your success (or lack thereof).

Make sure you understand the deadlines you have to hit in advance of getting to work with your client. Then make sure you can reasonably meet those deadlines, and build them directly into your SOW as part of your agreement. Whatever deadlines you agree to, make sure you stay on track with them or clearly communicate with your client in advance if you feel like you're getting off track.

The Dos and Don'ts of Contracts and SOWs

The truth is, many freelancers have found themselves on the wrong side of a poorly thought out contract or agreement, and it's never a pleasant experience. As a freelancer, you most likely won't have the same protections in place that businesses have. You probably won't have access to lawyers, or the cash flow necessary to recover your losses if you invest substantial time, effort, and money into a project. That's why protecting yourself as a freelancer is so important.

We can give some tips to get you pointed in the right direction...

Dos:

- Clearly state your duties and deliverables (be specific).
- Make sure to get legally binding signatures. You can use a digital document signing tool like docusign.com.
- Include clear and reasonable deadlines for your deliverables.
- Make sure you can actually meet those deliverables.
- Use a contract template and adapt it for your needs (don't reinvent the wheel).

Don'ts:

- Don't be vague. Vague terminology leaves room for scope creep.
- Don't forget to add dependencies (things that must happen first in order for your deliverables to be completed).
- Don't allow oral modifications to the contract during your project.
- Don't assume the client understands everything in the SOW or contract. Go over it together to get on the same page.
- Don't include items that you can't reasonably accomplish with your available resources.

Now let's dive into what may be the single most important aspect of your relationship with your client, and what may be the biggest factor of all in client retention.

Deliver Results and Show Progress

You have to actually deliver results for your clients or they won't stick around. Tracking, delivering, and reporting on results is how you will build confidence and trust in your relationship. Remember that your client is most likely seeing your relationship as an investment in their business, meaning that they are hoping for some kind of return on that investment.

For example, if you're a freelance social media manager and you're managing an Instagram page for a client, your client probably doesn't care about getting likes on Instagram posts. They're actually interested in how those likes will translate into some kind of positive return on their investment in you. They want to see how growth from their social media channels translate into growth for their business.

That's why having a game plan to deliver real results and show your progress to your client is key to keeping them around (and paying you).

Deliver Real Results and Always Add Value

What does it mean to add value? As a freelancer, it means delivering results for your clients that bring a return on their investment in you.

Therefore, step one of getting this right is to define what "results" actually mean in your contract. Make sure you both clearly understand what results mean in the context of your agreement. Otherwise, your relationship might begin to suffer as you deliver results that aren't up to the expectations of your client. Your client may have a substantially different idea of what results mean from what you plan on delivering.

Let's take an online lead generation campaign as an example.

To your client a lead might mean, "a decision maker in our target market with a real need for our services, and full details: name, email, phone number, business name, etc."

But to you a lead might simply mean, "someone who submits a form requesting more information, and leaves their name and email address."

See where this can start to really go off track with your client?

You might send them a ton of "leads", but if they don't meet your clients' expectations, and none of them convert into business for that client, you're on the rocks.

So how can we avoid this kind of stuff early on?

Step # 1 - Make sure you define what "results" actually means in your campaign (in the case of this example, a lead). Define that in your contract, and make sure your client has signed off on that definition.

Step # 2 - Make sure you can actually deliver those results at a price point that not only delivers value for your client, but leaves some profit for you - before signing the contract!

To take it even deeper, you want to be continually improving those leads so they feel that their investment is growing. Maybe you can improve the quantity or the quality of the leads, or find ways to make it easier for your client to close those leads. As a freelancer with no employee contract, justifying your ongoing relationship with the client is critical to ongoing success. And that leads us to tracking your progress.

Track Progress

Tracking progress is a critical function of your freelance business. Remember earlier we mentioned that it's good to create a regular communication schedule with your client for reporting on progress. Showing progress in the form of results daily, weekly, or monthly is a great way to keep your client happy and confident in your relationship. You don't want to get into a situation where your client has to come asking you for deliverables, or wondering why they haven't heard from you in a while.

Set up a simple way to show and track results, then commit to a timeframe to deliver those. An easy and free way to do this is with Google Spreadsheets. Create a simple reporting spreadsheet, and then fill it in and deliver updates as you go.

Here's an example for lead generation:

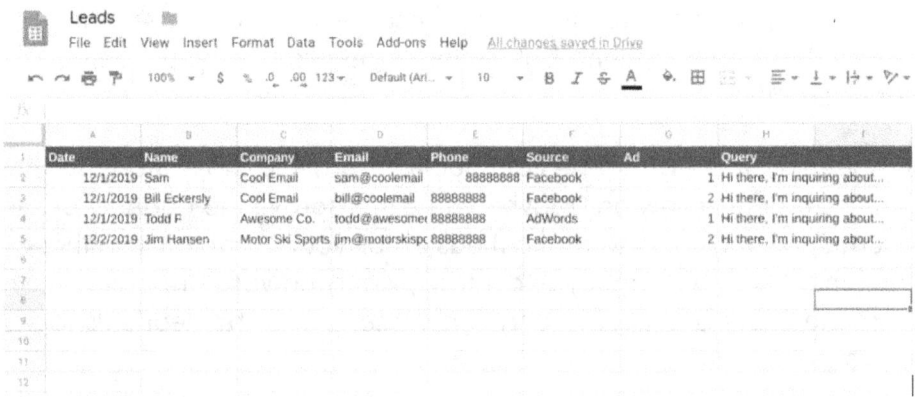

Now if you want to save yourself a bunch of time, you can automate this process with tools like Zapier.com or hire a virtual assistant to track progress. While this is a very simple example, the point is to illustrate that you can find an easy way to deliver results without creating a ton of extra work or headaches for yourself.

Learn When To Say "NO"

It's tempting early on in your freelance career to say "YES" to everything, but that might get you in trouble down the road. Saying yes to everything puts you in the precarious position of having to deliver on everything you've said yes to, even if you have no idea how to do those things.

Let's say you agree to build a website for a client on WordPress, but you have zero experience with WP. Competitors online are charging $500.00 for a simple 4-page site with no content. So you charge the same amount. What could possibly go wrong?

You get to work and find that the learning curve with WordPress is massive, and 30 hours into the project you're tearing your hair out in frustration. Now your hourly is WAY below your base rate and you've burned through a week. Most things you approach will be harder than they appear on the surface, and only experience will tell you what you can really accomplish with your unique skill sets.

This all comes down to being the expert; own the things you can reasonably do, and steer away from anything you know will put you in hot water. Your client relationships won't suffer by saying NO. In fact, if you do it right, this will help your relationships in the long run.

By setting boundaries, you're establishing great expectations with your client for future work, and paving the way for success.

Definitions

Marketing

Marketing is currently defined by the American Marketing Association (AMA) as "the activity, set of institutions, and processes for creating, communicating, delivering, and exchanging offerings that have value for customers, clients, partners, and society at large".

Internet marketing

Internet marketing (also known as online marketing, e-marketing, or web marketing,) is an all-inclusive term used to describe marketing activities conducted online.

Social media marketing

Using Facebook, Instagram, Twitter, LinkedIn, and similar social networks to create impressions on social media users over time.

Search engine optimization (SEO)

SEO is the process of optimizing content on a website so that it appears in search engine results.

Search engine marketing

It's also called "pay-per-click. This is a bit different than SEO, which is described above. Businesses pay a search engine to place links on pages of its index that get high exposure to their audience.

Video marketing

Video Marketing is creating and publishing all kinds of videos that entertain and educate their core customers

Marketing Evolution

Marketing evolution refers to the distinct phases that businesses have gone through as they continued to seek new and innovative ways to achieve, maintain and increase revenue through customer sales and partnerships.

Digital Marketing

Digital marketing, also called online marketing, is the promotion of brands to connect with potential customers using the internet and other forms of digital communication. For example, email, social media, and web-based advertising

Relationship marketing

Relationship marketing is an approach that focuses on encouraging customer retention and loyalty as well as continued interaction with the brand.

Digital Media

Digital Media Refers to audio, video, photo or textual content that has been encoded using a computer or smart device and can be transmitted digitally to people.

Email Filtering

A technique that organizes emails based on a word or phrase in an effort to keep the user's inbox free of spam – used to steer clear of spam filters and avoid blacklisting; allows targeted reach.

Influencer

an individual with a large following, such as a celebrity, industry expert, or content creator–in exchange for exposure

Freelancing

Freelancing is a type of self-employment. Instead of being employed by a company, freelancers tend to work as self-employed, delivering their services on a contract or project basis.

Keyword Stuffing

The practice of using too many keywords in the content to improve visibility on search engines.

Key Performance Indicator-KPI

A metric or quantitative benchmark to track progress towards marketing goals.

Engagements

Metrics to track the involvement of the customers with a brand's content for instance, number of likes, comments, and shares or interactions with videos, updates, blogs, etc.

CPC or Cost Per Click

A critical digital marketing metric showing how much a business pays for someone to click on their ad.

Target Audience

The group of people who could benefit from a company's offers

Scope creep

Scope creep simply means that the scope has got out of control and that ultimately the project has become undeliverable.

References

1. https://www.brafton.com/blog/content-marketing/evolution-of-marketing/
2. https://en.wikipedia.org/wiki/Marketing
3. https://mailchimp.com/marketing-glossary/digital-marketing
4. https://www.marketingevolution.com/marketing-essentials/what-is-a-digital-marketing-platform-marketing-evolution
5. https://techgeek365.com/power-digital-marketing/
6. https://n26.com/en-eu/blog/what-is-freelancing
7. https://www.mygreatlearning.com/blog/digital-marketing-tools/
8. https://digitalmarketinginstitute.com/blog/traits-of-a-successful-digital-matketing-professional
9. https://www.simplilearn.com/digital-marketing-terms-article
10. https://emeritus.org/blog/how-to-become-a-freelance-digital-marketer/
11. https://www.smartinsights.com/digital-marketing-strategy/8-reasons-digital-marketers-to-train-in-negotiations/
12. https://www.upwork.com/resources/freelance-digital-marketing-career-guide
13. https://www.teamwork.com/blog/freelance-digital-marketing/
14. https://thrivethemes.com/freelance-digital-marketing/freelance-operations/
15. https://thrivethemes.com/freelance-digital-marketing

16. https://blog.hubspot.com/marketing/what-is-marketing

www.ingramcontent.com/pod-product-compliance
Lightning Source LLC
Chambersburg PA
CBHW080502220526
45465CB00006B/2354